POOR LAW U
RECORDS

3. South-West England, The Marches and Wales

Jeremy Gibson and Colin Rogers

Federation of Family History Societies

Published 1993 by the
Federation of Family History Societies,
c/o The Benson Room, Birmingham and Midland Institute,
Margaret Street, Birmingham B3 3BS, England.

ISBN 1 872094 62 7

Computer typesetting in Arial, layout and cartography by Jeremy Gibson.
Cover graphics by Linda Haywood.
Cover illustration: from George Cruickshank's 'Oliver asks for more', in Charles
Dickens' *Oliver Twist*.

Printed by Parchment (Oxford) Limited.

Acknowedgements
Once again our deepest gratitude goes to the archivists who have responded so
conscientiously to yet another questionnaire, especially as this one was about
records often voluminous and not fully catalogued. In more than one record office the
response has been to spend time and energy on preparing such catalogues, and we
hope these will prove as useful on the spot as they have to us.

Amongst individuals we would like to thank Simon Fowler at the Public Record
Office and Colin Harris at the Bodleian Library; Professor Michael E. Rose for
reading our Introduction; Stella Colwell for allowing us to reprint much of her succinct
description of PLU records from her admirable *Dictionary of Genealogical Sources in
the Public Record Office*; and John Blight for lending, for far longer than longer than
he had expected, the atlas to the 1845 edition of Lewis's *Topographical Dictionary of
England*.

This is the first new Guide to benefit from the acquisition of a new computer
providing much closer control over typesetting and presentation. Jeffrey Long, Kevin
Tombs, Gerry Gracey Cox and Bob Boyd have all ungrudgingly given up valuable
time to quelling the birth pangs of its use.

J.S.W.G., C.D.R.

CONTENTS

INTRODUCTION

The Old Poor Law

Poor Law Unions were the invention of the late seventeenth century. The Poor Law Acts of 1597 and 1601, and the Act of Settlement of 1662, had placed the responsibility for poor relief firmly in the hands of each parish, whose unpaid overseers of the poor had to collect rates from occupiers of land and property, and spend income on helping the destitute, apprenticing their children, setting the unemployed able bodied to work, and if necessary having them conveyed back to their own parish of settlement. The absence of a national poor rate was one of the factors which determined the shape of poor law policy until well into the twentieth century.

This reliance on the parish as the administrative unit was first seen to have its limitations in the towns whose economic unity contrasted sharply with the numerous closely adjoining parishes within them, and in 1696 Bristol was allowed by Act of Parliament to have a joint Union workhouse, for its nineteen parishes. The advantages of the workhouse system – entry therein could replace the offer of external or 'outdoor' relief, so it became the workhouse or nothing for the destitute – was soon realised by other places; Unions were established in a number of towns across the south of England during the next quarter of a century (listed in S. and B. Webb, 1927/1963, pp. 120-1) and Knatchbull's Act of 1723, allowing individual parishes to hire premises for the same purpose, did not prevent others from following suit.

Over time, however, workhouses proved to be expensive – more so than giving outdoor relief, and Gilbert's Act of 1782 allowed Unions (each under a Board of Guardians) to give such relief to the able bodied while retaining workhouse places for the aged and infirm. Further liberalisation followed – from 1795, no one was to be removed under the Settlement Laws unless they were healthy, and had applied for relief, and support could be given even to those refusing admission to a workhouse. The Speenhamland system of 1795, recognising a sliding scale for outdoor relief which related to the price of grain, was only one such device by which individual parishes or Unions recognised the need to relate the level of financial assistance to the prevailing economic circumstances. Some relief was given in the shape of assisted passage for emigrants.

There were several problems for the development or even continuation of this system. The desire to offer outdoor relief in exchange for work directed by the poor law authority was thwarted by a lack of opportunity for such labour; some recipients were seen to be paid for being idle, and employers were believed to pay deliberately low wages, knowing that the balance of a living wage would be made up by the parish or Union. A significant number of the poor, particularly immigrants, were unassisted because of the Settlement Laws; on the other hand, in the eyes of many employers and economists, too many potential labourers were being removed from a free market. Expenditure on poor relief was perceived to be out of control, being related to demand rather than supply.

5

The New Poor Law of 1834

It seems a singular irony that the reforming Whig government of the 1830's should have introduced a piece of legislation which, even at the time, seemed one of the most draconian in our modern history. The paradox is one between the intent and the effect of 1834, not between 1834 and other measures. The enemy was not seen as poverty (which was merely a shortage of money, an ineradicable feature of a stratified society), but pauperism, a character defect involving idleness, unreliability, drunkenness etc., which led so many of its victims into desperate financial straits, and threatened the stability, if not the fabric, of society. Paupers were encouraged to breed by the very financial support which had been given in outdoor relief for the previous half century, and it was this belief, coupled with the ever increasing demands on ratepayers, which led the new government to set up a Royal Commission in 1832, on whose report the New Poor Law was based.

The Commission devised a simple way to eradicate pauperism at minimum cost and bureaucratic intervention – the system itself, an institutional stimulus-response experiment in utilitarianism, would compel the indigent to reform in order to avoid conditions in the workhouse which were to be deliberately worse than that of an 'independent labourer of the lowest class', a principle known as 'less eligibility'. Outdoor relief was to be phased out within two years, and paupers accepting indoor relief were to be made to feel like unwelcome guests.

The Act of 1834 implementing these recommendations was to be enforced by a national Commission which was to compel the formation of Poor Law Unions, each the responsibility of a Board of Guardians (partly ex-officio and partly elected by ratepayers). The Board appointed permanent officers, principally the relieving officer and workhouse master, supervised the activities of those officers, and spent the poor rates, normally through a committee structure. This included removal under the Settlement Laws (some 15,000 p.a. still being removed up the First World War), or paying other Unions to maintain 'their' paupers. The rates were still estimated according to the demands on each parish until 1865, when a Union rate replaced them. The Guardians remained until 1930; the Commission became the Poor Law Board in 1847, the Local Government Board in 1871, and was part of the Ministry of Health from 1919.

There was, of course, considerable resistance to the new scheme, whose workhouses were often referred to as 'bastilles'; in some parts of the industrial north, indeed, the very creation of Boards of Guardians was delayed for years, and even then, the intention of 1834 was subverted by Guardians unwilling to implement it (see Cole, 1984, Introduction). The extent of the effectiveness of the anti-Poor Law movement, however, has been questioned by Karel Williams (1981) who asserts that in those areas, outdoor relief to able bodied male adults was cut, being available from 1842 only as a reward for unpleasant tasks assigned by the Guardians, leaving an increasing number with no assistance at all. It certainly seems to be the case that this class, for whom 1834 was really intended, never formed anything like a majority of those being granted indoor relief. By the 1860's, all Unions had workhouses, usually of the 'general' kind in which all inmates were housed, regardless of age, sex, or reason for being there.

In addition to a hostile public opinion, the Victorian Guardians had to face recurrent problems over which they had little control. Unemployment in the cotton industry during the so-called 'cotton famine' (1862-65) was closely followed by the 'Lancet' scandal of 1865 which revealed the dreadful state of some of the medical wards in workhouses as dirty and poorly managed. Increasing criticism from socialists (through the Fabian Society) and others culminated in the famous published surveys by Charles Booth in London (from 1889) and Rowntree in York (1901) which demonstrated the true causes of poverty as unemployment, underemployment, the death of a wage earner in the family, or having large numbers of children – indigence as a character trait did not even appear as a category. The gradual enfranchisement of the working classes gave opponents of the system a stronger political foothold, and from 1894 the property qualification to become a member of a Board of Guardians was abolished.

The weakness of the 'pauperism' theory underlying the New Poor Law had been recognised by the Charity Organisation Society, founded in 1869, which divided the poor into 'deserving' (who should be treated by charitable organisations) and 'undeserving', for whom the poor law was designed. After 1871, there was an increasing specialisation in Union institutions, recognising that the 'general' workhouse could not adequately cater for those whose circumstances were radically different from each other -- the infirm, the aged, the sick, the children, the lunatics, and the unemployed. Children, for example, were raised in cottage homes in many Unions. The amount spent on out relief fell as this specialisation increased.

With hindsight, it seems astonishing that the New Poor Law should have survived well into the twentieth century,and can only be understood if it is recognised that its functions became increasingly vestigial as the years went by. From 1834, it might be viewed as a catch-all welfare system in which the Guardians had to treat all those who could not maintain themselves, and, because of this breadth of clientele, the Guardians were given responsibilities seemingly removed from the Poor Law itself. From 1836, for example, they had to oversee civil registration, and from 1853, sanitation and vaccination. From 1877, in areas without a School Board, they oversaw school attendance; and, from 1897 outside London, infant life protection. They housed youngsters in detention following the 1908 Children Act. Often, Union infirmaries dealt with cases from the population at large, especially during the First World War.

However, the growing conviction that functionalism – i.e., that different functions of welfare should be the responsibility of different agencies – was more effective led to the successive withdrawal of these functions from the Guardians. London hospitals took over in 1867; the School Boards and, later, County and Borough Councils gradually gained responsibility for the education of all children after 1870. Unemployment began to be countered by labour exchanges from 1909, and insurance rather than the workhouse from 1911. The Old Age Pension was introduced in 1908, and health insurance in 1911. There was, however, always something left for the Guardians to do.

Given these changes, both Majority and Minority reports of the Royal Commission on the Poor Laws, 1905-1909, advocated the abolition of the Guardians, and the virtual full employment during the First World War meant that they were becoming 'increasingly irrelevant'. However, the tidal wave of unemployment in the early 1920's ensured a continuing role, albeit as a backstop to the new insurance schemes which quickly spent the surplus which had accumulated during the war. Neither the Guardians nor the state had an adequate answer to unemployment on such a scale, and the 643 Boards of Guardians were abolished on 1 April 1930, though the Poor Law itself, including the Act of Settlement, lingered on until 1948.

The Records

We know of no single guide describing the contents of all the Union records, and it is clear that titles as well as contents might vary somewhat with time and place.

Union Records in the Public Record Office

As the main class of interest, **MH 12**, consists of 16,741 volumes (most of 500 to 1,000 pages) arranged by county (alphabetically) and within each county, by Union (alphabetically), the description, with precise references under each Union, is confined to 'Corres. etc. 1834-1900'. In the case of many Unions, this must be the major (sometimes only) nineteenth century source. It is certain to include names of countless individuals and some lists (for instance for sponsored emigration of paupers), particularly for the earlier decades.

MH 12 is described by Stella Colwell in her *Dictionary of Genealogical Sources* (page 52) as follows:

'Correspondence from the Boards and local authorities with the Poor Law Commission to 1847, and its successor, the Poor Law Board, and papers including applications for posts as Relieving Officer, schoolteacher, chaplain, medical officer, master and matron of the workhouse, embracing curriculum vitae, testimonials from previous employers or friends, letters of appointment, resignation and dismissal, vaccination records, details of lunatic inmates, examinations of paupers seeking help, provision for emigration, and information on outbreaks of infectious diseases. Within each Union records are arranged chronologically.'

MH 12 is indexed by subject in **MH 15**. However, the entries are very specialised and give no names or localities, so the indexes are unlikely to be of any use to family or local historians.

Post-1900 correspondence is continued in **MH 68**, but many volumes were destroyed during the Second World War, and the references are not provided in this Guide.

The other class referenced here under individual Unions in **MH 9**. Its volumes (arranged by Unions, or London districts, in alphabetical order) contain details of staffing, listing every officer employed in whatever capacity, dates of appointment and departure (with reasons for leaving) and their salary. The paid officers of one typical Union, Banbury in Oxfordshire, at various times included clerk, treasurer, chaplain, medical officers, master, matron, schoolmaster and mistress, porter, nurse, assistant in vagrant wards, assistant matron or superintendent nurse, many assistant nurses, tailor, clerk to School Attendance Committee, school attendance officers, inquiry officers, medical and relieving officers (by place) and vaccination officers (by district). The class list suggests these cover from 1837 to 1921. In fact, some appointments date from as early as 1835, but many Unions do not appear to have had full-time staff before the 1850's or 1860's. The date of the earliest appointment can be misleading, as this may be that of part-time staff, such as clerk, chaplain, baker, schoolmaster or mistress. The overall dates are usually given under each Union, but the register must be consulted to discover when a staffed workhouse actually became established. Further staff appointments, 1834-50 (not referenced here), are in **MH 19**.

Other 'Poor Law' classes are described as follows:

MH 14: plans of land and buildings, listed alphabetically by Union, 1861-1918; **MH 19/22**: correspondence with Government Offices concerning emigration of the poor, 1837-76; **MH 64**: official sanction permitting expenditure on assisted emigration of the poor, and for casual vacancies on the Boards of Guardians, 1916-32; **MH 32**: correspondence of Assistant Poor Law Commissioners and Inspectors, arranged alphabetically by name and reporting on workhouse conditions, 1834-1904; **MH 33**: registers of MH 32 correspondence, 1834-46; **MH 27**: correspondence between Poor Law Boards and Poor Law School Districts for administration and control of schools, appointment of managers, teaching and nursing staff, 1848-1910; **MH 18**: Visiting Officers' diaries concerning Metropolitan Casual Wards of vagrants, some containing dates of death of officers, and applications for vacant posts, 1874-78, 1881.

Census returns of staff and inmates in Union workhouses will be found in the decennial censuses from 1841 on (available at present to 1891).

There is an excellent introduction to the series by K.M. Thompson (1987). The calendar of the **MH 12** series is published in List and Index Society *Ministry of Health Poor Law Union Papers* vols. **56**, *(Bedford - Kent)*, **64**, *(Lancashire - co. Southampton)*, **77**, *(Stafford - Yorkshire - Wales)*. This shows the years covered by individual volumes of the series for each Union, but provides no additional information to that given here.

Union records in County and other local Record Offices

The main records generated by the Unions themselves concerning their day to day operations, where they survive, are held locally. Records of the Poor Law Guardians are sometimes the most voluminous series in a record office, reflected in this, the most extensive in the 'Gibson Guides' series so far. They are of interest to a wide variety of historians, economic, social, and political. Their very size, and the order in which the items are contained, have made them difficult to use, and they are therefore among the most under-exploited of major sources still to be opened up for personal or historical investigation.

The fullest description appears to be that in the published handlist to the Somerset Poor Law records, which was, we understand, the first to devise a classification for this type of record, but which has been expanded and clarified in the classification which follows. Several other record offices have published guides to their collections, often including an introduction to the records themselves. We have not followed this classification order in the Guide itself, as it had been devised for archival, rather than historical, use. What we call category 'A' records, those with substantial numbers of names of the general public or inmates, are given below in **bold type**.

Clerk to the Guardians

Board and Officers: Lists of members; service registers, acceptances, standing orders, superannuation returns, declarations of office, attendance books.

Minutes: Board of Guardians (**occasionally with lists of inmates**), in later years sometimes printed; Committees (e.g. finance, (work)house, boarding-out (**sometimes with lists of children**), relief etc.

Accounts (uniform nationally from 1848): Annual or half-yearly accounts were sometimes printed, and may include **names of those relieved**; Ledgers (general, treasurer's, parochial (till 1927), non-settled and non-resident poor (from 1845 only));

Petty cash;
Returns of paupers relieved (quarterly);
Financial statements (some statutory);
Precepts for, and statements of expenditure (incl. out of loans);
Poor rate returns;
Claims for grants in aid of poor rate expenditure (agricultural land, maintenance of pauper lunatics, repayment of salaries of teachers in poor law schools, and medical officers);
Loans granted to paupers (incl. name, parish, cause of loan, date, length, repayment);
Maintenance of indoor paupers in institutions of other authorities.

Lunacy: Maintenance;
Statements of conditions;
Registers of clothing;
Register of lunatics in asylums;
List of lunatics not in asylums;
Return of pauper lunatics (from 1842, name, age, sex, where maintained, and cost).
Statistics: Returns (weekly, fortnightly, monthly, half-yearly and annual; **weekly can include names**);
Miscellaneous returns, incl. pauper children;
Pauper classification book.
Case Papers: **Case papers on each person relieved, incl. dependents.**

Out-relief

Relief order book (applicant, parish, amount and period);
Register of non-resident and non-settled poor (name, residence, Union amount etc.);
Register of relief granted on loan;
Report of relief granted to aliens (1914-20);
Receipts of rent of pay stations.
Workhouses and Children's Homes: Buildings and provision documents (maps, supplies, contracts).
Supplies: Tenders.
Mortgages: Register of mortgages for loans on security of rates.
Children: **Register of children under control of the Guardians** (from 1889);
Indentures of apprenticeship of pauper children (from 1844);
Register of apprentices (from 1844) **and children placed in service** (from 1851);
Records of children apprenticed or employed;
Register of children boarded-out;
Reports by boarding-out visitors;
Accounts of maintenance of boarded-out children;
Miscellaneous files relating to boarding-out.
Irremovability, Settlement and Removal: Reports of removable and irremovable poor;
Settlement journey book;
Records of examination on application for removal orders;
Orders of adjudication and removal;
Consent to receive paupers without justices' order.
Recovery of relief: **Agreements by relatives to contribute**;
Orders for contributions by relatives.

Appointment of overseers: Appointment documents.
Statements received for preservation:
Overseers' balance sheets;
Rate collectors' monthly statements;
Orders for maintenance under the Bastardy Act 1845.
Miscellaneous: **List of paupers**;
Correspondence.

Treasurer

Treasurer's books and accounts.

Workhouse Master

Regulations: Regulations for the conduct of institution and staff;
Admission and discharge book (names, dates, occupation, age, religion, parish, cause of need of relief, class of diet; occasionally indexed, with full list of inmates, parish of settlement etc.);
Register of admission without orders;
Register of admission and discharge to workhouse school;
Register of admission refused;
Register of births in the workhouse (baptismal name, date of birth, sex, name(s) of parents, from what parish admitted, when and where baptised);
Register of baptisms in the workhouse;
Register of deaths in the workhouse (name, age, date of death, from what parish admitted, where buried);
Register of burials;
Register of sickness and mortality;
Register of apprentices and servants placed from the workhouse (date, master's name, trade and residence; sometimes age and parents);
Indoor relief list (name, date of birth, 'calling', creed, number of days in the workhouse; sometimes indexed; compiled every six months from admission and discharge books);
Medical examination books (inmates, children, alleged lunatics);
Workhouse medical relief book (name, age, date in sick ward, diet, when discharged etc.);
Records of lunatics in workhouse (register, detention certificates, register of mechanical restrant, notice to coroner of deaths, post-mortem books);
Medical Officer's reports on mental or bodily disease (lists and general reports);

Register of inmates;
Creed register (from 1876; name, date of birth, date and place of admission, creed, source of information, date of discharge or death; some give occupation, last address, name and address of nearest relative);
Individual record cards;
Leave of absence book;
Labour book;
Loans to paupers (mainly to pay for funerals);
Certificates of employment of pauper nurses and of inmates in sick wards;
Register of inmates' own clothing;
Register of applications and complaints by inmates;
Bathing register;
[Offences and] punishment book (name, date, offence, punishment by Master and Guardians);
Register of addresses of paupers' next of kin and friends;
Notices of illness or death to next of kin or friends.
Reports: Porter's book (sometimes lists visitors and reasons for visits);
Porter's admission and discharge book;
Report books of chaplain, matron, nurse, fire brigade;
Master's report book or journal (from 1842);
Report books of various visiting committees: general, lunatics, children, ladies etc.
Accounts: Master's day book;
Master's receipt and payment book;
Salaries and wages receipt book;
Officers' allowance account;
Workhouse minor accounts: baking, farm, garden, pig, oakum, stone, wood, bedding, crockery, linen, coffin, provisions, 'necessaries' and miscellaneous (tobacco, snuff etc.), heating, lighting, cleaning, clothing;
Order/requisition books;
Inventory books;
Dietaries (general, children's etc. by class);
Drug stock book.
Relief to casual poor: Register of wayfarers received;
Admission and discharge of casuals (date, hour, names of family, age, occupation, where slept previous night, cash in hand, work done during stay, where going next);

Records of ex-servicemen passing through casual wards;
Dietary table for casual poor.
Miscellaneous: Correspondence;
Receipts and expenses for workhouse.

Officer in charge of children's home
Indoor relief list;
Admission and discharge book;
Superintendent's report book;
Visitor's report book;
Inventory;
Provisions and necessaries accounts.

Relieving officer
Out relief lists (1834-47, with abstracts);
Out relief book (or relief order books 1848-1911; name, number, address, amount of relief, period);
Relief order lists (1911-30);
Abstracts of application and report (1834-47);
Application and report book (from 1847; name, age, date, address, length of stay, occupation, marital status; if a child, orphaned/deserted/illegitimate; if disabled, whether seeking medical relief, cause for seeking relief, date of visits to pauper's address, amount of relief ordered; some early ones might give place of settlement, ages of wife and children, names of relations liable for help, how long resident);
Receipt and expenditure book (from 1847; surnames only);
Diaries;
Orders for medical relief;
Pauper description book/list (names of applicant and family, address, year(s) of birth, disability, marital status, occupation, place of settlement, date first chargeable, present cause of relief, names and occupations of dependents);
Orders on tradesmen for relief in kind;
Out-relief lists of vagrants;
Relief to aliens' wives (1914-19; name of wife, address, number of children, amount given);
Miscellaneous forms and reports;
Register of visits to young persons under 16 hired or taken as servants from workhouse (name, age, date of hire, name and residence of master/mistress, trade, date of present and previous visits, whether servant was satisfied by position).

District Medical Officer
DMO relief book/list (name, age, parish, disease/accident, diet, treatment, fitness for employment);
DMO report book.

Collector of the Guardians
Collector's ledger;
Statement of arrears;
Receipt and payment book.

Non-poor law statutory duties
Civil registration: Returns of births and deaths;
Marriage notice books;
List of buildings registered for marriage;
Census plans etc.;
Correspondence;
Census register of children (name, residence, date of birth, present and previous school if any).
*Vaccination:*Vaccination committee minute books;
Vaccination registers;
Vaccinators' registers (name, date and place of birth, sex, name of father (or mother if illegitimate), father's occupation, when registered, date and recipient of vaccinator's notice, date of successful vaccination, or 'insusceptability');
Vaccination officer's report book;
Returns to central authority;
Contracts with public vaccinators;
Prosecution papers (from 1867).
Assessment: Assessment committee books;
Rate books;
Valuation books/lists (usually address, value, owner and tenant);
Returns of assessable values;
Correspondence, appeals etc.

Sanitation: Inspector of Nuisances report book;
Rural Sanitary Authority minute books (from 1872);
Allotments Committee books;
Bye-laws;
Ledgers, incl. parochial;
Clerk's petty cash book;
Medical Officer's reports;
Receipt and expenditure returns;
Register of common lodging houses;
Correspondence and miscellaneous.
School attendance: School Attendance Committee minute books (1877-1903);
Register of exemption certificates;
School Attendance Officer's reports;
Medical Officer's reports on school children;
School fees application and report book (name, date, age, relationship of applicant to child, number and ages of children under 16, applicant's age, address, occupation, marital status, if disabled, weekly earnings, name of school, length there, fee, and period ordered);
School fees order book;
School fees receipt and payment book;
Correspondence and miscellaneous.
Infant life protection: **Register of persons receiving infants**;
Register of infants received;
Inspector's reports on infants;
Notices to Guardians from persons retaining or receiving infants;
Notices to Guardians of removal of infant from care.

PRESENTATION

The following general points should be noted:

Whether or not closure is specifically mentioned in the text of the guide, it should be assumed that individual medical records are likely to be inaccessible to the public until they are one hundred years old. In many repositories records of individuals — just those of the greatest interest to family historians — are arbitrarily closed for any time up to a hundred years from the date of the last entry. This contrasts with the occasional printed reports which may include lists of paupers relieved, information that the Guardians of the time considered public property!

Bearing in mind the majority readership of the Gibson Guides, we have attempted to present the records in two groups. Group **A** (in bold in the foregoing list) are those records which contain large numbers of names of the public at the time, usually because they were in the workhouse or had applied for outside relief. Group **B** are therefore the rest, often including the names and details of those who worked for the Unions concerned.

Descriptions of records by title vary from one Union to another, and it is possible that, occasionally, one will be entered under the wrong category (**A** or **B**). We apologise in advance, and hope that users of the records will be able to alert the editors to such discrepancies.

Because of the pressure of space, we have not been able to include the reference numbers of the records themselves (except for those in the Public Record Office) and hope that record offices are not unduly inconvenienced by this. We have, for the same reason, excluded those records (such as copies of Acts of Parliament) which could be easily obtained elsewhere, and records which pertain only to one event or individual.

'Gaps' should be taken to mean that not all years are available between the dates stated.

'Part' implies that the record is not available for the whole of the Union.

'Various' indicates that there are both gaps in the series, and also that the whole Union is not covered.

Numerous abbreviations have been used throughout the Guide. They are listed inside the front cover.

Further reading and references

A. Benton, 'Sponsored migration under the New Poor Law', *Oxfordshire Family Historian* **2**.9 (1982) and *Midland Ancestor* **6**.8 (1983).

J. Cole, *Down poorhouse lane: the diary of a Rochdale workhouse* (Introduction) (1984).

J.A. Coleman, 'Guardians' minute books', *History* **48** (1963).

S. Colwell, *Dictionary of genealogical sources in the Public Record Office* (1992).

M.A. Crowther, *The Workhouse system, 1834-1929* (1981).

A. Digby, *The poor law in nineteenth century England and Wales* (1982).

A. Digby, *Pauper palaces* (1978) (with special reference to Norfolk).

S. Fowler, 'Records of Poor Law Unions held in the Public Record Office', *History*, in 'Short Guides to Records' series (forthcoming).

D. Fraser, *The new poor law in the nineteenth century* (1976).

P. Harling, 'The power of persuasion: central authority, local bureaucracy and the New Poor Law', *English Historical Review* **107** (1992).

N. Longmate, *The workhouse* (1974).

P. Mandler, 'Tories and paupers: Christian political economy and the making of the New Poor Law', *The Historical Journal* **33** (1990).

P. Mandler, 'The making of the New Poor Law *redivivus*', *Past and Present* (1987).

R. Noschke and R. Rocker, 'Civilian internment in Britain during the first world war', *Anglo-German Family History Society* (1989).

P. Riden, *Record Sources for Local History* (1987) (pp 112-117).

M.E. Rose, *The English poor law 1780-1930* (1971).

M.E. Rose, *The relief of poverty 1834-1914* (1972, 1986).

M.E. Rose, *The poor and the city: the English poor law in its urban context, 1834-1914* (1985).

W.B. Stephens, *Sources for English local history* (2nd edition, 1981).

K.M. Thompson, 'Sources for the New Poor Law in the Public Records', *Journal of Regional and Local Studies* **7**.1 (1987).

R. Vorspan, 'Vagrancy and the New Poor Law in late-Victorian and Edwardian England', *English Historical Review* **92** (1977).

S. and B. Webb, *English poor law policy* (1910/1963).

S. and B. Webb, *English poor law history: part 1 – the old poor law* (1929); *part 2 – the last hundred years* (1929).

K. Williams, *From pauperism to poverty* (1981).

P. Wood, *Poverty and the workhouse in Victorian Britain* (1991).

MAPS

The figures in square brackets after each Union heading identify their location on the county maps. These are based on the maps in the 1845 edition of Lewis's *Topographical Dictionary of England* and the companion work on *Wales*. Although most of the country was already unionised, there were, as mentioned in the Introduction, places which still resisted this requirement. In most counties it has been possible to identify such areas with the Unions they eventually became. The only major area to defy such identification is a large swathe of the West Riding of Yorkshire, where it has been necessary to leave the boundaries of the many eventual Unions of this populous area undefined. It must also be borne in mind that after 1845 further Unions were created out of existing ones, or boundaries changed. The maps are there to give an idea of the geographical location of Unions (and civil registration and census districts), especially those overlapping county borders, but, even for 1845, are not guaranteed as accurate.

The places which made up each English Union at any time are shown in the Gazetteer which is Part 4 of this Guide, based on the information given in F.A. Youngs, jr., *Local Administrative Units of England* (Royal Historical Society, 1981, 1991). The Gazetteer also shows the places constituting each Union in Wales (including Monmouthshire) at the time of the 1851 census.

BERKSHIRE

The PLU in which each parish lay is shown in the Berkshire volume of the *National Index of Parish Registers*, **8**, 1 (Society of Genealogists, 1989); and also, for north-western Berkshire (Vale of the White Horse), now in Oxfordshire, in C.G. Harris, *Oxfordshire Parish Registers and Bishops Transcripts*, (Oxfordshire F.H.S., 4th edition, 1993).

Except when shown otherwise, records are at **Berkshire Record Office**, *Reading*. See *Guide to the Records of the New Poor Law*, Berkshire Record Office, 1984.

Abingdon [3] (partly in Oxon.).
A. Settlement papers 1883-1924; lunacy 1893-1928; adm. and discharge reg's 1916-30; order for adm. to casual ward 1920; deaths reg. 1866-94; valuation lists (Abingdon, Dry Sandford, Shippon) 1862-95; vac. reg's 1883-1910.
B. Min's 1835-39, 1844-1930; C'tee min's: Assessment (and Chairman's) 1862-1927, SAC 1888-1903; C'tee reports: Finance and Gen. Purposes 1917-30, Visiting and House etc. 1890-1930, RSA 1872-94; ledger 1928-30; stat. of ac's 1836, 1844; stat. returns of paupers 1892; financial statement 1917; corres. 1894-1930; conveyance of w'h. papers 1836-1902; provisions contracts 1930; ag'mts for boarding-out children 1879-1921; sup'an. reg. 1897-1915; treasurer's cash book 1928-30; ac's: clothing, materials, hardware 1908-32, provisions consumption 1928-31, farm 1928-32; Infant Life Protection Act report book 1907-12; w'h. dietaries 1836.
Public Record Office, Kew:
Corres. etc. 1834-1900 [MH 12/139-59]; staff reg. 1837-1921 [MH 9/1].

Basingstoke [10] (Stratford Mortimer, until 1866). See under Hampshire.

Bradfield [8] (partly in Oxon.).
A. Reg. of affiliation orders 1853-64; MO's relief book 1912-19; school adm. reg. 1850-56; lunacy 1921-30; adm. and discharge reg's 1835-62 (vagrants 1848-1917); relief lists 1845-1921; creed reg's 1872-1905; births reg. 1836-62; deaths reg. 1835-42; information against paupers 1835-46; porter's books 1911-29; relief order books 1835, 1848-1930; parochial tithe book 1866-68; vac. reg's 1871-81; valuation list (Tilehurst) 1879-80.
B. Min's 1835-1929 (missing 1867-71, 1874-84, 1904-07); C'tee min's: Central W'h. 1835-49, House 1895-1901, 1913-30, Boarding-out 1911-29, Children's Act 1913-16, Contracts 1914, RSA 1873-88; letter books 1835-1922 (gaps); ledgers 1880-95; parochial ledger 1888-92; corres., PLC and LGB 1820-1912; weekly returns to PL inspector 1854-5; w'h. papers, spec's etc. 1835-60; leases of Theale parish property 1820-37; ag'mts for use of w'h.

accommodation 1927-30; treasurer's cash book 1928-9; boarding-out ag'mt (Hungerford Union) 1921; service book 1851-1911; chaplain's report book 1908-17; master's reports and journals 1855-57, 1913-21; daily diets 1915-22; bread, provisions, necessaries ac's 1866-81, 1904-24; clothing ac's 1903-24; RSA min's 1873-88, ledgers 1873-84.
Public Record Office, Kew:
Corres. etc. 1834-1900 [MH 12/162-79]; staff reg. 1837-1921 [MH 9/3].

Cookham [13] (renamed Maidenhead 1899).
A. Adm. and discharge books 1836-50 (vagrants 1848-9); indoor relief lists 1836-42, 1854-1932 (gaps); births reg's 1836-68; deaths reg's 1836-67; outdoor relief appl's 1835-37; appl. and report book (Waltham St. Lawrence) 1840-1; relief order book 1848-1930.
B. Min's 1835-42, 1847-1930; Assessment C'tee min's 1881-1901; reg. of securities 1870-1925; weekly outdoor relief lists 1836-43.
Maidenhead Library.
'Poor Law relief in Maidenhead District (1632-1899): a report on old documents accumulated at the Poor Law Institution, Maidenhead' by J.W. Walker and H.E. Bannard, December 1918; Maidenhead Union Shopkeepers' Receipts, late C19 to 1910, incl. some burial receipts.
Public Record Office, Kew:
Corres. etc. 1834-1900 [MH 12/181-99]; staff reg. 1837-1921 [MH 9/11, as Maidenhead].

Easthampstead [14].
A. Births reg's 1849-1914; deaths reg's 1848-1914.
B. Min's 1870-75, 1880-1930; RSA min's 1882-88, 1893-4; ledger 1928-30; ag'mt for use of casual ward by Joint Vagrancy C'tee, with corres. 1927-8; treasurer's cash book 1927-30.
Public Record Office, Kew:
Corres. etc. 1834-1900 [MH 12/201-16]; staff reg. 1837-1921 [MH 9/6].

Faringdon [2] (partly in Oxon., Glos.).
A. Lunacy 1914-30; vagrants' adm. and discharge books 1916-7, 1921-33; births reg's 1835-1932; baptisms reg. 1927-33; deaths reg's 1875-1933.
B. Min's 1835-1930; Assessment C'tee min's 1862-1912; ledger 1927-30; papers on transfer of Faringdon w'h. erected c.1801 under Gilbert's Act 1801-36; licence and papers on w'h. chapel 1848; sale of cottages, Fernham 1874-76; receipts for stocks, draft mortgage 1843-1914; collector's ledger 1927-29; garden, pig, firewood ac's 1917-34.
Public Record Office, Kew:
Corres. etc. 1834-1900 [MH 12/217-32]; staff reg. 1837-1921 [MH 9/7].

Henley-on-Thames [11] (Remenham). See under Oxfordshire.

Berkshire continued

Hungerford (and Ramsbury) [4] (partly in Wilts.).

A. MO's relief books 1875-1906, also Lambourn 1927-34, Great Bedwyn (Wilts.) 1916-21, Ramsbury (Wilts.) 1919-26; reg. of servants and appr's (incl. children of school age, sent to orphanages) 1877-.1917; births reg. 1866-1914.
B. Min's 1835-1930; C'tee min's: Standing and Special 1922-27, Assessment 1862-93, RSA 1872-94; House C'tee reports 1914-30; letter book 1843-48; ledger 1926-30; ac's for building Union 'poor house' 1835; papers on loans for financing erection of w'h. 1848-52; and drainage there 1912-39; corres. on valuation of w'h., for rating, 1915; contracts for building work 1923-28; and goods 1930; reg. of securities 1912-26; guarantee policy for clerk 1891-1923; sup'an. reg. and reg. of salaries 1894-1930; treasurer's cash book 1928-9; collector's ledger 1919-30.
Public Record Office, Kew:
Corres. etc. 1834-1900 [MH 12/234-51]; staff reg. 1837-1921 [MH 9/9].

Maidenhead see **Cookham.**

Newbury [7].

A. Relief book 1913-16; boarding-out reg. 1896-1930; lunacy 1925-30; adm. and discharge books 1866-75; porter's adm. and discharge books 1911-22; creed reg's 1894-1928; births reg. 1868-1909; baptisms reg. 1836-68; deaths reg's 1868-1909, 1914-43; valuation lists: general 1896, individual places (Boxford, Brimpton, Chieveley, Cold Ash, Enborne, Greenham, Hamstead Marshall, Midgham, Newbury, Speen, Thatcham, Welford, Winterbourne) various periods between 1883 and 1918; vac. reg. 1906-09.
B. Min's 1835-1930; C'tee min's: House 1920-30, Finance 1921-25, RSA 1872-94, Assessment 1862-1927, SAC 1877-1907, Boarding-out 1927-30; standing orders c.1836; letter books (indexed) 1847-94; PLC corres. etc. 1834-41; returns to PLB 1838-50; list of guardians and officers 1842-3; w'h. building plans etc. 1835-58, 1928-9; chapel licence 1836; papers re. sales of property (Greenham, Brimpton) 1836, 1842-56; allegations of ill treatment of children 1852; ag'mt re. transfer of Newtown (Hants.) to Kingsclere Union 1895; ag'mt etc. re. maintenance of boys on training ship Exmouth 1896-98; contracts for provisions 1840-43, 1913; ledgers 1898-1930; financial statements 1881-92, 1901-07; treasurer's cash books 1906-13, 1927-30; ac's etc. for Boarding-out C'tees (Welford and Speen) 1896-1923; inventory 1929; firewood ag'mts 1898-1938; Master's receipts and payments 1914-5.
Note. Further records have recently been deposited at Berkshire R.O., but are not yet catalogued and in any case may remain closed.
Public Record Office, Kew:
Corres. etc. 1835-1900 [MH 12/252-73]; staff reg. 1837-1921 [MH 9/12].

Reading [9].

B. Min's 1835-1930; C'tee min's: Finance 1910-30, General Purposes 1919-30, W'h. Infirmary Casual Ward Visiting 1910-30, House Revision 1911-14, Infant Poor 1910-22, Building and Farm 1912-30, Dispensary 1913-29, Stores and Furnishing 1917-30, Assessment 1905-16; ledgers 1920-30.
Public Record Office, Kew:
Corres. etc. 1834-1900 [MH 12/275-94]; staff reg. 1837-1921 [MH 9/14].

Wallingford [6] (partly in Oxon.).

A. Cottage Homes relief lists 1901-24 and adm. and discharge book 1908-10; births reg. 1909-45; deaths reg. 1909-42; punishment book 1907-46; outdoor relief lists (1st Dist.) 1894-1924; appl. and report books (Cholsey Dist.) 1897-1925; relief order book 1914-5; supplemental valuation list 1892-97; Ewelme (Oxon.) valuation list 1897-1902; vac. reg's (Cholsey and Dorchester, Oxon., Dist's) 1888-1917; tithe assessments 1873-88.
B. Min's 1835-1930; C'tee min's: House 1917-32, Women's 1914-22, Cottage Homes 1900-20, Boarding-out 1917-23; PLB letters 1842, 1852, 1854; weekly return to PL inspector 1921-23; ledger 1929-30; ac's 1929; reg. of securities 1891-1926; sup'an. reg. 1914-27; MO's report book 1901-12; provisions consumption ac's 1919; parochial investments reg. 1846-99.
Public Record Office, Kew:
Corres. etc. 1834-1900 [MH 12/297-314]; staff reg. 1837-1921 [MH 9/18].

Wantage [5].

A. Boarding-out reg's 1906-19; w'h. school attendance reg. 1890-94; lunacy 1924-49; births reg's 1836-1913; deaths reg's 1835-66; vagrants' adm. and discharge reg's 1914-28; punishment book 1911-19; vac. reports and reg. 1872-1925.
B. Min's 1835-1930 (1865 missing); financial statements 1927-30; plans etc. re. alterations, additions to w'h. 1906-29; ledger 1928-30; sup'an. reg. 1910-19; cash book 1922-27; ag'mt for joint use of union school at Cowley (Oxon.) 1922; casuals' report book 1925-36; visitors' book 1911-21; inventories, 1924-40; garden and pig ac's 1892-1930; scattered homes: daily meals 1917-19.
Public Record Office, Kew:
Corres. etc. 1834-1900 [MH 12/318-33]; staff reg. 1837-1921 [MH 9/18].

Windsor [15] (partly in Surrey).

A. Relief lists 1915-30; relatives' addresses 1879-1927; deaths reg's 1835-48, 1867-88, 1908-32; 1938; porter's books 1914-18; pauper service book 1877-1914.complaints reg. 1916-40; punishment books 1867-1938; porter's books 1914-18.
B. Min's 1873-91, 1894-1930; House C'tee reports 1914-5, 1926-7; letter books 1910-27; ledgers 1913-30; reg. of securities 1896-1924; medical and welfare service book 1877-1914; master's reports 1883-1926; oakum ac's 1899-1927; Assessment

Berkshire: Windsor *continued*

C'tee min's 1902-16 (also New Windsor parochial 1837-40).
Public Record Office, *Kew:*
Corres. etc. 1834-1900 [MH 12/335-59]; staff reg. 1837-1921 [MH 9/19].

Witney [1] (Shilton, until 1844).
See under Oxfordshire.

Wokingham [12].
A. Outdoor relief appl. and report books 1894-1917; relief order lists 1896-1930; vac. reg. 1902-23.
B. Min's 1835-1930; House C'tee reports 1921-29; Ladies' Visiting C'tee min's 1880-1930; plan of w'h. 1848; contracts etc. on additions and alterations 1909-30; spec. etc. children's cottage homes, Oxford Road, Wokingham 1911-2; ag'mt for use of casual wards 1927; ledgers 1915-30; treasurer's ledgers 1916-27; collector's ledgers 1894-1932.
Public Record Office, *Kew:*
Corres. etc. 1834-1900 [MH 12/362-78]; staff reg. 1837-1921 [MH 9/19].

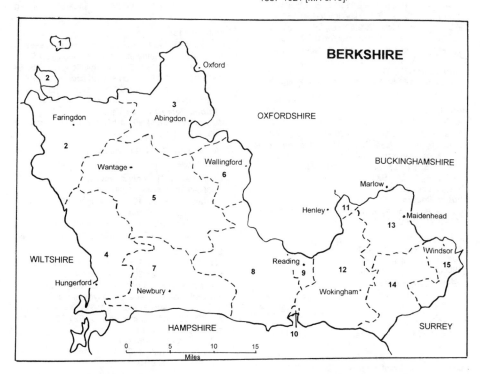

CORNWALL

See B. Wellington, 'Public opinion and the introduction of the New Poor Law in Cornwall', *Old Cornwall* 9 (2 parts, 1979, 1980).

Except when shown otherwise, records are at **Cornwall Record Office**, *Truro.*
Records less than 75 years old are closed to the public.

St. Austell [9].
B. Min's 1839-43, 1845-48, 1890-92, 1897-1930; Boarding-out C'tee min's 1921-29; ledgers 1905-15, 1918-29; parochial ledger 1913-27; collector's ledgers 1911-22, 1927-29; sup'an. ledger 1896-1930; treasurer's ac's 1920-22; reg. of mortgages 1895-1916; House C'tee reports 1926-29; quarterly statements of repayments 1903-24; salary reg's 1919-30; officers' salary reg. 1889-1922.
Public Record Office, Kew:
Corres. etc. 1834-1900 [MH 12/1245-69]; staff reg. 1837-1921 [MH 9/1].

Bodmin [5].
A. Relief order book 1930.
B. Min's 1842-44, 1877-81, 1884-87, 1896-1930; ledgers 1884-87, 1891-1927; parochial ledger 1915-30; treasurer's ac's 1916-24; Children's Boarding-out C'tee min's 1912-23; SAC min's 1901-03; officers' salaries reg. 1878-1929; sup'an. reg. 1896-98; statement of ac's 1898.
Public Record Office, Kew:
Corres. etc. 1834-1900 [MH 12/1274-95]; staff reg. 1837-1921 [MH 9/3].

Camelford [3].
A. Relief order book 1930.
B. Min's 1879-1930; ledgers 1873-76, 1884-1930; treasurer's ledger 1928-30.
Public Record Office, Kew:
Corres. etc. 1835-1900 [MH 12/1299-1312]; staff reg. 1837-1921 [MH 9/4].

St. Columb Major [8].
A. Deaths reg. 1914-30; relief order book 1900; adm. and discharge book 1926-33.
B. Min's 1837-68, 1871-1930; ledgers 1837-81, 1884-1927; parochial ledgers 1852-59, 1861-67, 1874-96; treasurer's ledger 1922-29; reg. of securities 1904-27; staff reg. 1848-1904; receipt and exp. book 1930; letter book 1888-92; master's report book 1897-99; House C'tee report book 1922-25.
Public Record Office, Kew:
Corres. etc. 1834-50, 1858-1900 [MH 12/1313-32]; staff reg. 1837-1921 [MH 9/5].
See also Padstow.

Falmouth [12].
B. Min's 1839-1930; ledgers 1837-64, 1869-76, 1880-1930; parochial ledgers 1852-1917, 1920-26; non-settled poor ledgers 1903-30; service reg's 1901-30; Children's Home C'tee min's 1928-30; treasurer's ac's 1923-30.

Public Record Office, Kew:
Corres. etc. 1834-66, 1871 Sep.-1900 [MH 12/1337-59]; staff reg. 1837-1921 [MH 9/7].

St. Germans [7].
A. Vac. reg. 1920-25; Union cases book 1837-61.
B. Min's 1837-39, 1891-95, 1911-30; C'tee min's: Children's Home 1919-29, Finance 1924-29, Relief 1930-32; ledgers 1856-60, 1909-17, 1920-26; receipt and exp. book 1923-26; quarterly salaries reg. 1913-17; treasurer's ac's 1920-30; porter's book 1894-5.
Public Record Office, Kew:
Corres. etc. 1834-1900 [MH 12/1364-80]; staff reg. 1837-1921 [MH 9/7].

Helston [13].
B. Min's 1850-94, 1901-30; C'tee min's: Assessment 1862-92, Settlement 1903-15; ledgers 1837-73, 1878-82, 1886-1929; parochial ledgers 1856-64, 1880-87, 1896-1913; non-settled poor ledger 1898-1930; reg. of salaries 1927-29; master's half-yearly report 1914.
Public Record Office, Kew:
Corres. etc. 1834-96 [MH 12/1384-1403]; staff reg. 1837-1921 [MH 9/8].

Holsworthy [2] (North Tamerton).
See under Devon.

Launceston [4] (partly in Devon).
A. Relief order book 1930.
B. Min's 1890-94, 1908-30; ledgers 1890-1927.
Public Record Office, Kew:
Corres. etc. 1834-1900 [MH 12/1407-26]; staff reg. 1837-1921 [MH 9/10].

Liskeard [6].
B. Min's 1894-1929; C'tee min's: Finance 1920-29, Boarding-out 1923-30; ledgers 1904-12, 1914-22; non-settled poor ledger 1912-30; maintenance ledger 1915-30; quarterly repayment statements 1927-29; treasurer's ledgers 1922-28; service reg's 1855-1929; financial statements 1921-23; reg. of securities 1899-1914.
Public Record Office, Kew:
Corres. etc. 1834-1900 [MH 12/1429-49]; staff reg. 1837-1921 [MH 9/10].

Padstow (pre-1834; later in **St. Columb Major**).
B. Ag'mts between Padstow w'h. proprietors and overseers of 31 other parishes or places for their paupers to be admitted to w'h.; w'h. ac's 1769-88, 1795-1800.

Penzance [14].
A. Reg. of indoor cases 1920.
B. Min's 1837-1930; ledgers 1905-27; parochial ledgers 1910-27; C'tee min's: Finance 1907-13, 1916-19, 1922-30, House 1914-22, 1927-30, Removal of Children 1910-14, Assessment 1896-1916, Visiting 1903-14, Boarding-out 1922-30; salaries book 1919-30; service reg. 1890-1928.

Public Record Office, *Kew:*
Corres. etc. 1834-1900 [MH 12/1453-78]; staff reg.
1837-1921 [MH 9/13].

Plympton St. Mary (St. Budeaux).
See under Devon.

Redruth [11].
A. Indoor relief lists 1837-1930 (gaps); adm. and
discharge books 1840-1934 (gaps); creed reg's
1910-30; deaths reg's 1837-67, 1901-39; index of
inmates c.1912-24; offences and punishment book
1914-47; medical relief book 1849-51; DMO's relief
lists 1880-88; medical case papers 1910-18; reg. of
children boarded-out 1910-20.
B. Min's 1855-1930; C'tee min's: General 1854-76,
Assessment 1862-80, Finance 1921-30; Visitors'
(lunacy) 1882-1909, Lunacy 1926-30, Boarding-out
1911-25, 1927-30; ledgers 1837-1929; parochial
ledgers 1851-1929; treasurer's ac's 1915-30;
master's receipt and exp. books 1911-42; general
ac's books 1851-55, 1859-68; relieving officer's ac's
1922-25; casual paupers' daily provisions ac's 1914-
5; provisions consumption ac's 1917-8; financial
statements 1868-89; master's report books 1842-
1928 (gaps); master's journal 1911-17; visitors'
books 1837-1914 (gaps); reg. of visitors 1861-63;
Visiting C'tee book (lunacy) 1882-1909; House C'tee
report book 1914-22; inventory books 1850-71,
1877-1908, 1915-36; letter book 1850-58; diet
sheets 1926; service reg's 1883-1929; additionally,
a large number of misc. administrative and financial
papers, incl. vac. and epidemics, school attendance.
Cornish Studies Library, Redruth:
A. Indoor and outdoor paupers 1913-4, 1926 (incl.
inmates at Mental Hospital, Bodmin).
B. Statements: half-yearly 1912-22, yearly 1923-7.

Redruth *continued*

Public Record Office, *Kew:*
Corres. etc. 1834-1900 [MH 12/1486-511]; staff
reg. 1837-1921 [MH 9/14].

St. Austell see under '**Austell**'.
St. Columb Major see under '**Columb**'.
St. Germans see under '**Germans**'.

Isles of Scilly.
Although listed by Youngs as a PLU, no records
are known, nor is there any mention of the Isles of
Scilly in Penzance PLU records. These do however
record payments to the 'overseers of Scilly'. Poor
relief was administered via a Select Vestry, for which
minute books from 1832 on are held in the Town
Hall, St. Mary's, Isles of Scilly.

Stratton [1].
B. Min's 1869-1929; ledgers 1902-30; parochial
ledger 1907-26; letter book 1929-30.
Public Record Office, *Kew:*
Corres. etc. 1835-42, 1856-1900 [MH 12/1516-25];
staff reg. 1837-1921 [MH 9/16].

Tavistock (Calstock).
See under Devon.

Truro [10].
B. Min's 1857-1930; ledgers 1857-66, 1875-1914,
1916-28; treasurer's ac's 1915-25; service reg.
1896-1911; reg. of officers' salaries 1928-9; SAC
min's 1877-1903; Boarding-out C'tee min's 1925-30;
House C'tee reports 1914-30.
Public Record Office, *Kew:*
Corres. etc. 1834-1899 [MH 12/1527-52]; staff reg.
1837-1921 [MH 9/17].

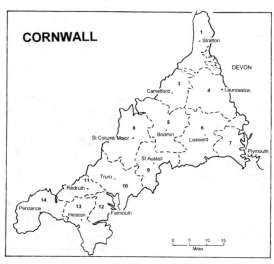

DEVON

Axminster [14] (partly in Dorset).
Devon Record Office, Exeter:
B. Min's: Guardians 1836-1932, Boarding-out C'tee 1910-32, Assessment C'tee 1903-18; treasurer's ledgers 1926-32.
Public Record Office, Kew:
Corres. etc. 1834-1900 [MH 12/2095-120]; staff reg. 1837-1921 [MH 9/1].

Barnstaple [1].
North Devon Record Office, Barnstaple:
A. Collector's receipts and payments 1845-1950.
B. Min's 1855-59, 1870-75, 1878-1927; C'tee min's: Boarding-out 1912-32, Assessment 1887-1925, SAC 1877-1903, House 1910-32; treasurer's ledgers 1929-32.
Public Record Office, Kew:
Corres. etc. 1834-83, 1886-1900 [MH 12/2124-55]; staff reg. 1837-1921 [MH 9/2]

Bideford [2].
North Devon Record Office, Barnstaple:
B. Min's 1929-32; Assessment C'tee min's 1904-27; letter books 1907-09, 1916-39.
Public Record Office, Kew:
Corres. etc. 1834-1900 [MH 12/2166-87]; staff reg. 1837-1921 [MH 9/2].

Chard [13] (Yarcombe).
See under Somerset.

Crediton [7] (formed by Act of Parliament, 1697).
Devon Record Office, Exeter:
Pre-1834: W'h. min's 1757-8, 1778, 1792; ac's 1756, 1770-78; day book 1830-33.
B. Min's 1836-1932; Boarding-out C'tee min's 1912-32.
Public Record Office, Kew:
Corres. etc. 1834-1900 [MH 12/2193-214]; staff reg. 1837-1921 [MH 9/5].

Devonport see Stoke Damerel.

Dulverton (Morebath).
See under Somerset.

Exeter [22].
Devon Record Office, Exeter:
B. Min's (1834)-1930; ledgers 1857-1949; parochial ledgers 1879-1901.
Public Record Office, Kew:
Corres. etc. 1834-1900 [MH 12/2238-55]; staff reg. 1837-1921 [MH 9/6].

Holsworthy [5] (partly in Cornwall).
North Devon Record Office, Barnstaple:
B. Min's 1836-39, 1926-32; Assessment C'tee min's 1896-1932; treasurer's ledger 1921-32; ac's book 1924-30.
Public Record Office, Kew:
Corres. etc. 1835-1900 [MH 12/2258-71]; staff reg. 1837-1921 [MH 9/8].

Honiton [10].
Devon Record Office, Exeter:
A. Boarding-out C'tee reg. 1904-32.
B. Min's 1905-32.
Public Record Office, Kew:
Corres. etc. 1834-1900 [MH 12/2273-95]; staff reg. 1837-1921 [MH 9/9].

Kingsbridge [21].
Devon Record Office, Exeter:
B. Treasurer's ledger 1928-32.
Public Record Office, Kew:
Corres. etc. 1834-1900 [MH 12/2300-24]; staff reg. 1837-1921 [MH 9/9].

Launceston [15] (Broadwoodwidger, Northcott, North Petherwin, St. Giles on the Heath, Virginstow, Werrington).
See under Cornwall.

Molton, South [4] (partly in Som.).
North Devon Record Office, Barnstaple:
B. Min's 1895-98, 1911-20; Assessment C'tee min's 1888-1927; ledger 1929-31.
Public Record Office, Kew:
Corres. etc. 1834-1900 [MH 12/2493-516]; staff reg. 1837-1921 [MH 9/15].

Newton Abbot [17].
Devon Record Office, Exeter:
A. Letter book (births and deaths) 1836-38.
B. Mortgages (East Street) 1784-1905; deeds etc. 1765-1837, 1859, 1877-97; corres. 1836-42; building contract and ac's 1837; treasurer's ledger 1927-32.
Public Record Office, Kew:
Corres. etc. 1834-1900 [MH 12/2328-78]; staff reg. 1837-1921 [MH 9/12].

Okehampton [6].
Devon Record Office, Exeter:
A. Outdoor relief lists 1853-1914; appr. indentures 1921; removal orders 1868, 1883; appl. and report books 1906-16.
B. Min's 1836-1927; C'tee min's: Assessment 1862-1927, SAC 1900-03, fortnightly meeting 1865-70; letter book 1880-86; treasurer's ledgers 1836-1928; parochial ledgers 1880-1914; petty cash ledger 1848-55; relieving officer's ledgers 1914-16; financial statements 1904-10; w'h. plans (1900, ?1914); deeds etc. 1852-99, 1902-14; contracts for vac. 1877-1908; insurance and repair contracts 1908-39; RSA min's 1872-95, ledgers 1873-94.
Public Record Office, Kew:
Corres. etc. 1834-1900 [MH 12/2394-416]; staff reg. 1837-1921 [MH 9/12].

Plymouth [23].
West Devon Record Office, Plymouth (many records were destroyed by enemy action during 1941):
A. Police court summonses (indexed) 1896-1903, 1913-32; rate books 1818-20, 1832-3.

Devon: Plymouth *continued*

B. Board and C'tee min's (indexed) 1909-30; PLB, LGB corres. 1851-1915; ledgers 1829-1930; receiver's ledgers 1851-61; non-settled poor ledger 1915-30; relieving officer's ac's 1928-31.
Public Record Office, Kew:
Corres. etc. 1834-1900 [MH 12/2420-53]; staff reg. 1837-1921 [MH 9/13].

Plympton St. Mary [18].
Devon Record Office, Exeter:
A. Births and deaths reg. 1868-1917.
West Devon Record Office, Plymouth (see note under Plymouth):
A. Indoor relief lists 1837-1941; outdoor relief lists 1928-41; adm's and discharges reg. 1867-1929; births and deaths reg's 1868-1914.
B. Min's 1838-1929; C'tee min's: Assessment 1862-1923, House 1895-1929, Boarding-out 1916-30, SAC 1884-1903, Children's Homes 1911-29; treasurer's ledgers 1843-53, 1929-32; parochial ledgers 1857-1914; provisions ac's 1895-97.
Public Record Office, Kew:
Corres. etc. 1836-1900 [MH 12/2463-87]; staff reg. 1837-1921 [MH 9/13].

St. Thomas (by Exeter) [9].
Devon Record Office, Exeter:
A. Births and vac. returns 1906-15; RDC reg's of electors 1888-1927.

St. Thomas (by Exeter) *continued*

B. Min's: Guardians 1836-1931; C'tee min's: Special 1836-1903, Visiting 1879-1908, Assessment 1862-87, SAC 1888-1903; reg. of securities 1896-1904; Poor Law C'tee: rules and reg'ns 1836-48, corres. 1837-52; lease of w'h. property 1854; officers' bonds c.1869-1905; deeds 1836-54; treasurer's ac's 1928-9; ledger 1926-30; Guardians' and officers' statements 1837-1920; building fund ac's books 1845-1902; RSA orders etc. 1878-88.
Public Record Office, Kew:
Corres. etc. 1834-1900 [MH 12/2567-98]; staff reg. 1837-1921 [MH 9/17].

Stoke Damerel [23] (Devonport from 1897).
See A. Chiswell, 'Guardians of the Poor Minutes: 1836/7 Stoke Damerel', *Devon F.H.* **19** (July 1981).
West Devon Record Office, Plymouth (see note under Plymouth):
A. Non-settled poor ac's book 1915-30; receipts and exp. 1913-26.
B. Overseers' general ledger 1894, 1910-30 and cash books 1911-27; overseers' min's 1903-14; charity min's 1847-1941.
Public Record Office, Kew:
Corres. etc. 1834-1900 [MH 12/2517-32]; staff reg. 1837-1921 [MH 9/16 (Stoke Damerel), MH 9/6 (Devonport)].

Stonehouse, East [19].
West Devon Record Office, Plymouth (see note under Plymouth):
B. Overseer's ledgers 1886-1930 (gaps).

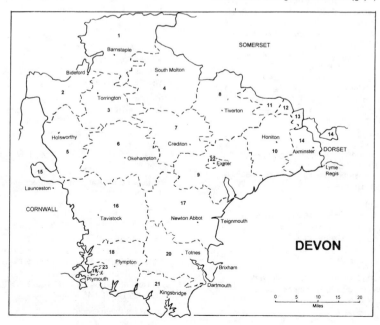

Devon: Stonehouse, East *continued*

Public Record Office, *Kew:*
Corres. etc. 1834-1900 [MH 12/2217-35]; staff reg. 1837-1921 [MH 9/6].

Taunton [12] (Churchstanton).
See under Somerset.

Tavistock [16] (partly in Cornwall).
Devon Record Office, Exeter:
A. Adm. and discharge reg. (casuals) 1922; births reg's 1866-1945; deaths reg. 1866-1919; children's reg. and relief list 1914-30; creed reg's 1868-75, 1879-90, 1914-32; punishment book 1914-48.
B. Treasurer's ledger 1926-32; reg. of mortgages 1894-98; reg. of contracts 1917-32.
Public Record Office, *Kew:*
Corres. etc. 1839-1900 [MH 12/2540-63]; staff reg. 1837-1921 [MH 9/17].

Tiverton [8].
Devon Record Office, Exeter:
Pre-1834: Court misc's 1747-76; adm. reg. 1767-76; treasurer's receipt and exp. book for w'h. 1699-1769.
B. Min's 1923-26; ledgers 1927-32; ac's book 1929-32.
Public Record Office, *Kew:*
Corres. etc. 1834-1900 [MH 12/2605-31]; staff reg. 1837-1921 [MH 9/17].

Torrington [3].
North Devon Record Office, Barnstaple:
A. Births reg. 1872-1935; deaths reg. 1871-1914; reg. of lunatics 1891-1922 (closed until 2023); birth/vac. returns 1871-76, 1880-1915; collector's receipts and exp. 1922-3; reg. of mechanical restraint 1890-1911; reg. of inmates' property c.1900; reg. of tramps 1914; appl's for lunacy cert's c.1899-1911; clothing book 1922-39; outdoor relief lists 1926-7; appl. and report books 1927-8; births/vac. returns 1872-1931, deaths 1881-1914.
B. Min's 1837-1932 (gaps); C'tee min's: Assessment 1862-1927, Boarding-out 1898-1932, RSA 1872-86; letter books 1910-25; stock records 1900-46; ledger 1925-30; sup'an. reg. 1887-1917; garden and pig ac's book 1904-43; master's half yearly reports 1915-46; MO's report book 1929-47.
Public Record Office, *Kew:*
Corres. etc. 1834-1900 [MH 12/2636-55]; staff reg. 1837-1921 [MH 9/17].

Totnes [20].
North Devon Record Office, Barnstaple:
B. Mortgage loan, 1915.
Public Record Office, *Kew:*
Corres. etc. 1834-1900 [MH 12/2656-93]; staff reg. 1837-1921 [MH 9/17].

Wellington [11] (Burlescombe, Clayhidon, Culmstock, Hemyock, Holcombe Rogus).
See under Somerset.

DORSET

See J. Smith, 'The workhouse and its records', *Dorset F.H.S.* **3**.3 (1990).

Except when shown otherwise, records are at **Dorset Record Office,** *Dorchester.*

Axminster [1] (Chardstock, Charmouth, Hawkchurch, Lyme Regis, Thorncombe).
See under Devon; see also **Thorncombe,** below.

Beaminster (pre-1836).
A. W'h. inmates (with dates of discharge) 1810-36; reg. of appr's 1804-18; children innoculated against smallpox 1812; families applying for relief 1816; children vac'd 1824, 1834; inventories of inmates' goods 1818-32.
B. W'h. ledger 1796-99; ac's 1796-1804, 1818-35; contracts 1827-8, 1833-35.

Beaminster [3] (partly in Somerset).
See also **Broadwindsor,** below.
A. Pauper offence book 1842-69.
B. Min's 1836-1930; C'tee min's: Assessment 1900-27, Boarding-out 1899-1930; ledgers: general 1929-30, Assessment C'tee 1923-26; w'h. building contract 1837.
Public Record Office, *Kew:*
Corres. etc. 1834-1900 [MH 12/2705-23]; staff reg. 1837-1921 [MH 9/2].

Blandford Forum (pre-1834).
A. Reg's of inmates 1761-75 (gaps), 1793, 1805; relieved indoor and outdoor poor 1854 (sic).
B. Ac's 1760-77; w'h. rules, early C19.

Blandford Forum [13].
B. Min's 1835-1930; Assessment C'tee min's 1862-1927; ledgers 1929-30.
Public Record Office, *Kew:*
Corres. etc. 1834-1900 [MH 12/2724-43]; staff reg. 1837-1921 [MH 9/2].

Bridport [4].
B. Min's 1836-1930; C'tee min's: School Attendance and Boarding-out 1900-30, Assessment 1862-1926, House 1924-26; ledgers 1909-30.
Public Record Office, *Kew:*
Corres. etc. 1834-42, 1849-56, 1860-1900 [MH 12/2744-60]; staff reg. [MH 9/3].

Broadwindsor (later **Beaminster**).
B. Ac's. 1791-1894.

Cerne Abbas (pre-1834).
B. Ac's 1808-18.

Cerne Abbas [6].
B. Min's 1835-1925; Assessment C'tee min's 1923-27; ledgers 1916-30; plans of PL w'h. 1836.
Public Record Office, *Kew:*
Corres. etc. 1834-1904 [MH 12/2764-76]; staff reg. 1837-1921 [MH 9/4].

Chard [2] (Wambrook).
See under Somerset.

Dorset *continued*

Christhurch.
See under Hampshire.

Cranborne.
1836 only. See with **Wimborne**.

Dorchester (pre-1838).
B. Min's and ac's 1743-1837.

Dorchester [7].
B. Min's 1900-30; C'tee min's: Assessment 1904-27, Boarding-out 1910-35; House C'tee reports 1914-27; ledgers 1928-30.
Public Record Office, Kew:
Corres. etc. 1834-53, 1860-71, 1875-1900 [MH 12/2777-91]; staff reg. 1837-1921 [MH 9/6].

Holdenhurst.
See under Hampshire.

Mere [9] (Bourton, Silton).
See under Wiltshire.

Poole [16].
See M.J. Flame, 'The politics of poor law administration in the borough of Poole 1835 - c.1845', *Dorset Nat. Hist. and Arch. Proc.* **108** (1986).
B. Min's 1835-1930; C'tee min's: House Management 1895-1930, Infirmary 1915-29, Finance 1917-29, Institution 1912-19; ledgers 1924-30; reg. of securities 1884-1913.
Public Record Office, Kew:
Corres. etc. 1834-71, 1876-79, 1885-1900 [MH 12/2797-815]; staff reg. 1837-1921 [MH 9/13].

Purbeck (1836 only).
See with **Wareham**.

Shaftesbury [12].
B. Min's 1835-1930; House C'tee min's 1914-30; SAC min's 1914-20; ledgers 1903-30.
Public Record Office, Kew:
Corres. etc. 1839-76, 1883-1900 [MH 12/2819-28]; staff reg. 1837-1921 [MH 9/15].

Sherborne [5] (partly in Somerset).
A. W'h. inmates' property reg. 1920-31.
B. Min's 1836-1930; SAC min's 1877-92; Visiting C'tee min's 1911-27; ledgers 1907-30; treasurer's ac's 1913-29; clerk's out letters 1852-62.
Public Record Office, Kew:
Corres. etc. 1834-59, 1867-1900 [MH 12/2830-44]; staff reg. 1837-1921 [MH 9/15].

Sturminster Newton [11].
Pre-1834: **B.** Ac's 1738-1833.
B. Min's 1891-1930; ledgers 1891-1930; plans of w'h. 1836, 1903.
Public Record Office, Kew:
Corres. etc. 1834-1900 [MH 12/2846-60]; staff reg. 1837-1921 [MH 9/16].

Thorncombe (later **Axminster**).
B. Ac's 1735-1809.

Wareham and Purbeck [14].
B. Min's 1836-1930; ledgers 1855-1930; parochial ledgers 1904-30.
Public Record Office, Kew:
Corres. etc. 1834-1900 [MH 12/2861-82]; staff reg. 1837-1921 [MH 9/18].

Weymouth [8].
B. Min's 1923-25; Assessment C'tee min's 1910-27; ledgers 1929-31.
Public Record Office, Kew:
Corres. etc. 1834-48, 1871-1900 [MH 12/2885-2901]; staff reg. 1837-1921 [MH 9/18].

Wimborne and Cranborne [15].
A. Baptisms reg. 1839-1914, 1920, 1929.
B. Min's 1835-1930; Assessment C'tee min's 1892-97; ledgers 1927-30.
Public Record Office, Kew:
Corres. etc. 1834-1900 [MH 12/2911-25]; staff reg. 1837-1921 [MH 9/19].

Wincanton [10] (Buckhorn Weston, Kington Magna).
See under Somerset.

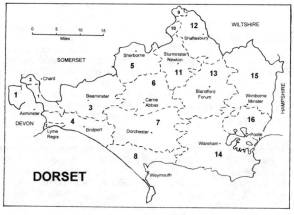

GLOUCESTERSHIRE and BRISTOL

Except when shown otherwise, records are at *Gloucestershire Record Office, Gloucester.* Daily charge payable.

Banbury [4] (Shenington, until 1844).
See under Oxfordshire.

Barton Regis see **Clifton.**

Bristol [25] (partly in Som.).
Bristol City Record Office:
Apparently no locally held records (?destroyed by enemy action in 1940), but see Clifton below.
Public Record Office, Kew:
Corres. etc. 1837-1900 (missing: 1848-57, 1874, Aug. 1880-81, Jan. - May 1900) [MH 12/3862-902]; staff reg. 1837-1921 [MH 9/3].

Cheltenham (pre-1834).
B. Deeds of w'h. 1799-1804.

Cheltenham [13].
A. Reg's of lunatics 1842-1931; reg. of children under control of guardians 1894-1931; appr. records 1845-1922; reg. of removals 1899-1908; reg. of maintenance cases 1905-22; adm. and discharge books 1835-1941 (gaps); births reg. 1836-56, 1908-14; deaths reg. 1836-51; indoor relief list 1912-47; reg. of inmates c.1900-35; children's home adm. and discharge books 1915-38; poor rates for Badgeworth, Charlton Kings, Cheltenham, Leckhampton and Prestbury 1836-1921 (sample only); valuation lists of Badgeworth, Charlton Kings, Cheltenham, Prestbury, Shurdington, Staverton and Swindon 1863-1940.
B. Min's 1835-1930; c'tee min's 1883-1930; ledgers 1835-1930; financial statements 1848-90; plans of w'h. alterations 1883-1912; letter books 1877-79, 1905-08, 1922; misc. papers 1835-77; chaplain's report book 1918-28; master's journal 1914-29; Assessment C'tee min's 1862-1933.
Public Record Office, Kew:
Corres. etc. 1834-1900 (missing 1848-49, 1863-65, 1877) [MH 12/3912-52]; staff reg. 1837-1921 [MH 9/4].

Chepstow [10] (Alvington, Aylburton, Hewelsfield, Lancaut, Lydney, St. Briavels, Tidenham, Woolaston).
A. Lydney out-relief order book 1921-27; valuation lists for Alvington, Aylburton, Hewelsfield, Lancaut, Lydney, St. Briavels and Tidenham 1911-12.
B. Assessment C'tee min's 1908-27.
Otherwise see under Wales: Monmouthshire.

Chipping Sodbury see under **Sodbury.**

Cirencester [18] (partly in Wilts.).
A. Valuations of Cirencester 1848, 1865-1927; Cirencester rate book 1914.
B. Min's 1836-1935; C'tee min's 1914-35, Assessment 1862-1927, SAC 1877-1901; ledgers 1870-1928; letter book 1853-60; visiting c'tee reports 1837-38.

Cirencester Bingham Library.
A. Lists of paupers (printed) 1878, 1880-1912 (also financial statements 1908-12).
B. W'h. plan 1837 (p'copy); lists of c'tee members 1909-10, 1926-7; description of life at Cirencester W'h. from *Sunday at Home,* Aug. 1890 (p'copy).
Public Record Office, Kew:
Corres. etc. 1834-1900 [MH 12/3980-97]; staff reg. 1837-1921 [MH 9/5].

Clifton ('Gilbert' workhouse).
Bristol City Record Office:
B. Min's etc. 1796-1805; mortgages 1757-83; deeds from 1548 (see below); contracts for passage to Van Dieman's Land 1833; ac's of poor children's pin work 1779-80; printed ac's 1796-7.

Clifton [24] (originally **Barton Regis** and reverted to this name in 1876; from 1902 with **Bristol**).
Bristol City Record Office (most records destroyed by enemy action in 1940; records less than 70 years old closed to public inspection):
A. Births reg. 1868-78, 1898-1943; deaths reg. 1847-1914, 1924-39; baptisms reg. (St. Thomas, Eastville) 1907-31; reg. of adopted children 1899-1931 (incl. lists of children over whom Guardians had control 1914-17); creed reg's 1869-1952; list of occupants in wards and children in infant school (n.d.); collector's receipt and payment book 1836-48.
B. Draft min's 1901-03; plans for altering St. Peter's Hospital 1898-9, 1913; deeds 1548-1902; printed ac's 1834-37, 1884-1901; RSA: min's 1894-1904, letter books 1896-1904, ledgers 1900-04.
Public Record Office, Kew:
Corres. etc. 1834-1906 [MH 12/4000-45]; staff reg. 1837-1902 [MH 9/5 (Clifton), MH 9/3 (Barton Regis)].

Dursley [21].
A. Out-relief order books 1848-56; births and deaths reg. 1866-1920; rate books for Coaley, Kingswood, Nympsfield, Stinchcombe, Wotton-under-Edge and Dursley 1895-1926; valuation lists of Cam, Coaley, Dursley, Kingswood, North Nibley, Nympsfield, Owlpen, Slimbridge, Uley and Wotton-under-Edge 1888-1927.
B. Min's 1836-1933; C'tee min's 1913-29, Assessment 1862-1924, SAC 1891-1903; w'h. building c'tee min's and papers 1836-39; ledgers 1896-1927; letter book 1887-93, 1924-28; master's journal 1842-48; visiting c'tee report books 1839-56; overseers' ac's for Cam 1899-1927, Kingswood 1923-27, Owlpen 1922-27, Slimbridge 1888-1909, Stinchcombe 1913-26, Uley 1923-27 and Wotton-under-Edge 1883-1906.
Gloucester Library:
A. Paupers (named), abstracts of parochial ac's (printed) 1892 (incl. RSA summary of nuisances), 1908-16.
B. Visiting C'tee min's 1830-34; PLC orders 1836.
Public Record Office, Kew:
Corres. etc. 1834-1900 [MH 12/4054-71]; staff reg. 1837-1921 [MH 9/6].

Gloucestershire *continued*

Evesham [1] (Ashton under Hill, Aston Somerville and Subedge, Child's Wickham, Hinton on the Green, Cow Honeybourne, Pebworth, Saintbury, Weston Subedge, Willersley).
See under Worcestershire.

Faringdon [27] (Lechlade).
See under Berkshire.

Gloucester [12].
A. Out-relief order books 1903-09.
B. Min's 1835-1930; ledgers 1835-1925; overseers' ac's: Gloucester 1901-27, Maisemore 1869-1928, Over, Higham and Linton 1908-28; w'h. master's report book 1929-32; Assessment C'tee min's 1862-1910, 1921-27; SAC min's 1877-1903; Union Year Books 1912-30; PLC circulars 1840-46; w'h. deeds 1799-1909 (see also Gloucester Borough, rating and valuation).
Gloucester Library:
A. Paupers (named), abstracts of parochial ac's (printed) 1875, 1893, 1908, 1912-3; paupers St. Mary-de-Lode 1859/60..
B. Min's (ptd.) 1911-30; Union year book 1906-7.
Public Record Office, Kew:
Corres. etc. 1834-1900 [MH 12/4073-107]; staff reg. 1837-1921 [MH 9/7].

Keynsham [26] (Bitton, Hanham (Abbots), Kingswood, Mangotsfield, Oldland, Siston).
See under Somerset.

Kingswood (near Wotton; formerly Wilts., later in Dursley).
B. Min's 1837-44.

Malmesbury [19] (Minety, until 1844).
See under Wiltshire.

Monmouth [9] (English Bicknor, West Dean, Newland, Staunton).
A. Poor rate books for Coleford, Newland, Staunton and West Dean 1873, 1914-26; valuation list, West Dean 1921.
Otherwise see under Wales: Monmouthshire.

Newent [8].
A. Adm. and discharge books 1835-1903; outdoor relief lists 1928-32; poor rate books for Bromsberrow, Corse, Dymock, Highleadon, Newent, Oxenhall, Pauntley, Preston, Redmarley d'Abitot, Rudford, Taynton and Upleadon 1888-1926; valuation lists for same places except Oxenham and Taynton, plus Hartpury, Kempley, Staunton, Tibberton and Aston Ingham (Herefs.) 1864-1927.
B. Min's 1835-1930; C'tee min's: Assessment 1862-1924, Nuisance Removal 1866, SAC 1877-1904; pay books 1909-21.
Gloucester Library.
B. Union enquiry report 1871.
Public Record Office, Kew:
Corres. etc. 1834-61, 1867-1900 [MH 12/4114-30]; staff reg. 1837-1921 [MH 9/12].

Northleach [14].
A. Poor rates and valuation lists for Aldsworth, Aston Blank, Gt. and Lit. Barrington, Bibury, Chedworth, Coln Rogers, St. Aldwyn and St. Denys, Compton Abdale, Dowdeswell, Eastleach, Hampnett, Hasleton, Northleach, Salperton, Sevenhampton, Sherborne, Shipton, Southrop, Stowell, Turkdean, Whittington, Windrush, Winson, Withington, Yanworth, Farmington and Eastington (nr. Northleach) 1896-1926.
B. Min's 1875-1937; C'tee min's: Assessment 1893-1927, SAC 1877, 1901-03; ledgers 1870-1911; letter book 1925-29; school attendance officer's reports 1878-1901.
Public Record Office, Kew:
Corres. etc. 1834-1900 [MH 12/4134-44]; staff reg. 1837-1921 [MH 9/12].

Ross [28] (Lea Bailey, Ruardean).
A. Poor rates for Ruardean, and for Linton and Upton Bishop (Herefs.) 1914-25.
Otherwise see under Herefordshire.

Shipston on Stour [3] (Admington, Batsford, Bourton on the Hill, Chipping Campden, Clopton, Ebrington, Hidcote Bartrim, Ilmington, Lower Lemington, Mickleton, Moreton in Marsh, Quinton, Todington).
See under Warwickshire.

Sodbury, Chipping [23].
A. Out relief list 1906-43; valuation list, Iron Acton c.1840.
B. Min's 1836-45, 1852-1930; ledgers 1921-30; superintendent registrar's min's, letter and ac's book 1845-57; Assessment C'tee min's 1884-1927.
Public Record Office, Kew:
Corres. etc. 1834-1900 [MH 12/3962-79]; staff reg. 1837-1921 [MH 9/5].

Stow on the Wold [7].
B. Min's 1836-99, 1903-15, 1920-24, 1927-35; ledgers 1846-1930; spec. for erection of w'h., with plan 1836.
Public Record Office, Kew:
Corres. etc. 1834-1900 [MH 12/4145-61]; staff reg. 1837-1921 [MH 9/16].

Stratford on Avon [2] (Clifford Chambers, Dorsington, Marston Sicca, Preston on Stour, Welford, Weston on Avon).
See under Warwickshire.

Stroud [17].
A. Poor rates for Nailsworth, Stroud and Uplands 1914-26; valuation lists as for poor rates, plus Rodborough and Thrupp 1905-27.
B. Min's 1836-1930; C'tee min's: Roxburgh House Boarding-out 1926-30, Assessment 1882-93; ledgers 1922-29; chaplain's report book 1847-91.
Public Record Office, Kew:
Corres. etc. 1834-1900 [MH 12/4164-91]; staff reg. 1837-1921 [MH 9/16].

Gloucestershire *continued*

Tetbury [22].

A. Out-relief order book 1912-16; DMO's relief books 1876-1928; vac. reg's 1893-1921; poor rate books and valuation lists for Ashley, Avening, Beverstone, Boxwell and Leighterton, Cherington, Didmarton, Kingscote, Long Newnton, Newington Bagpath, Ozleworth, Shipton Moyne, Tetbury Upton, Westonbirt and Lasborough and Tetbury 1862-1927.

B. Min's 1836-1917, 1924-30; C'tee min's: 1856-63, 1925-30, Assessment 1862-1927, SAC 1896-1903; ledgers 1836-1923; plans of proposed new w'h. 1904; overseers ac's: Ashley 1848-1912, Avening 1909-27, Boxwell and Leighterton 1914-27, Cherington 1910-27, Kingscote 1895-1918, Newington Bagpath 1909-27, Long Newnton 1903-27, Shipton Moyne 1911-27, Tetbury Upton 1914-27; corres. re. building of new w'h. 1904-08.

Public Record Office, *Kew:*

Corres. etc. 1834-1900 [MH 12/4196-204]; staff reg. 1837-1921 [MH 9/17].

Tewkesbury [5].

A. Out-relief order book 1898-1902; adm. and discharge reg's 1916-48; reg. of inmates 1911-1953; out-relief lists 1901-37; valuation of whole Union (except Ashchurch and Tewkesbury) 1897-1927 and of whole Union (except Chaceley) 1875-90.

B. Min's 1835-1930; ledgers 1888-1907; corres. 1885-1921; Visiting C'tee reports 1929-53; Tewkesbury Borough SAC min's 1877-93.

Public Record Office, *Kew:*

Corres. etc. 1834-88, 1891 May-1900 [MH 12/4205-22]; staff reg. 1837-1921 [MH 9/17].

Thornbury [20].

A. Out-relief order book 1909-11; rate and valuation books for Almondsbury, Alveston, Berkeley, Cromhall, Falfield, Hamfallow, Breadstone, Hinton, Littleton-on-Severn, Oldbury-on-Severn, Rangeworth, Rockhampton, Thornbury 1859-1926; Thornbury parish valuation 1841.

B. Min's 1836-1935 (gaps); C'tee min's: Boarding-out 1913-30, Assessment 1862-84, SAC 1877-80; House C'tee reports 1914-32; ledgers 1854-1930; financial statements 1879-90; letter books 1846-72.

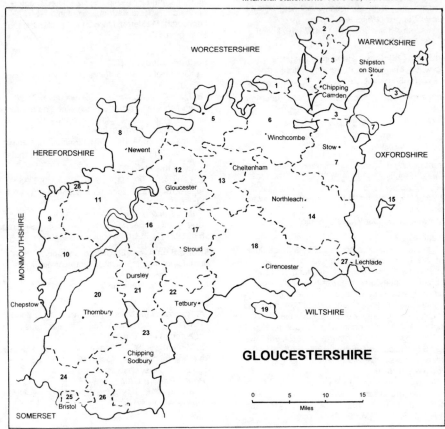

GLOUCESTERSHIRE

Bristol City Record Office (records less than 70 years old closed to public inspection):
A. Thornbury Hospital: births reg. 1847-65, 1924-48, deaths reg. 1866-1960, creed reg. c.1914-36; collector's receipts and payments 1892-97.
B. Thornbury Hospital: MO's reports 1917-39; papers re. poor relief collection c.1880-1930, Assessment C'tee min's 1884-1901.
Public Record Office, Kew:
Corres. etc. 1834-46, 1852-55, 1867-1900 [MH 12/4224-35]; staff reg. 1837-1921 [MH 9/17].

Uley.
B. Chaplain's and visitors' report books 1836-39.

Warmley (out relief).
B. Min's 1897-1930; c'tee min's 1910-34.
Gloucester Library:
A. Paupers relieved (printed) 1909.

Westbury on Severn [11].
A. Poor rates and valuation books for Awre, Blaisdon, Bulley, Churcham, East Dean, Flaxley, Huntley, Littledean, Longhope, Minsterworth, Mitcheldean 1894-1925.
B. Min's 1835-1955 (gaps); ledgers 1835-1930 (gap); plans of w'h. 1869; officers' service reg's 1850-1930.
Public Record Office, Kew:
Corres. etc. 1835-1900 (missing 1862-3, 1867-69, 1879-80) [MH 12/4236-59]; staff reg. 1837-1921 [MH 9/18].

Wheatenhurst [16].
A. Adm. and discharge reg. 1836-44; births reg. 1836-1913.
B. Min's 1835-1930; ledgers 1835-1930; plans for erection of w'h. 1870-74; letter book 1885-97; visitors' report book 1836-41; Assessment C'tee min's 1862-1927; SAC min's 1877-1903.
Gloucester Library:
A. Paupers relieved (printed) 1892-3.
Public Record Office, Kew:
Corres. etc. 1843-1900 [MH 12/4262-70]; staff reg. 1837-1921 [MH 9/18].

Witney [15] (Widford, until 1844).
See under Oxfordshire.

Winchcombe [6].
B. Min's 1836-1935; ledgers 1836-1911; master's journals 1848-1934; Visiting C'tee reports 1925-34; relieving officer's ac's 1836-38; Assessment C'tee min's 1862-1908.
Public Record Office, Kew:
Corres. etc. 1843-1900 [MH 12/4271-84]; staff reg. 1837-1921 [MH 9/19].

HAMPSHIRE (Co. Southampton)

Most records are at **Hampshire Record Office,** *Winchester.*

See *Poor Law in Hampshire through the Centuries: A Guide to the Records,* Hampshire Archivists Group Publication No. **1**, Hampshire C.C., 1970 (now very out of date; revised version of the section relating to Hampshire R.O. holdings (1991) for internal use available at Hampshire R.O.).

There is a restriction on public access to those records of w'hs and other institutions which mention personal names until 100 years after their date of completion. The following lists do not include rating or valuation papers.

Alresford [11].
Hampshire Record Office, Winchester:
B. Min's 1835-1918; Assessment C'tee min's 1862-1927; vac. officer's report books 1920-32.
Public Record Office, Kew:
Corres. etc. 1834-1900 [MH 12/10613-24]; staff reg. 1837-1921 [MH 9/1].

Alton [12].
Hampshire Record Office, Winchester:
A. Relieving officer's appl. and report books 1879-1932; outdoor relief lists and receipt and exp. books 1879-1936; DMO's relief books 1898-1921; valuation lists 1863-1922; vac. officer's reg. 1904-10; adm. and discharge books 1888-1942 (gaps); reg's of inmates, deaths, lunatics, maternity cases etc. 1849-1942; MO's report and exam. books and other records 1884-1940.
B. Min's 1842-1930; House C'tee min's 1914-32; ac's 1839-1931 (incl. ledgers 1839-1929); letter books 1879-90; relieving officer's notebooks c.1923-27; Assessment C'tee min's 1862-1927; vac. officer's report book 1874-85; master's reports and journals 1862-1940 (gaps); chaplain's report books 1877-1926; ac's (various) 1853-1942.
Public Record Office, Kew:
Corres. etc. 1834-1900 [MH 12/10625-42]; staff reg. 1837-1921 [MH 9/1].

Alton, Hartley Wintney and Farnham (Surrey) **District Pauper School, Crondall.**
Hampshire Record Office, Winchester:
A. Adm. and discharge reg. (boys) 1846-70; attendance reg's (boys and girls) 1852-96 (gaps).
B. Journals of instruction in industry 1850-53; school mistress's journal and report books 1846-50; porter's books 1851-54, 1870-73, 1975-78.

Alverstoke [31] (Incorporation 1799-1852; PLU from 1852).
Hampshire Record Office, Winchester:
B. Min's (and report books) 1799-1831, 1852-1930; c'tee min's 1910-30; ledgers 1861-66, 1920-27.
Portsmouth City Records Office:
B. Assessment C'tee min's 1912-27 (Alverstoke parish).

Public Record Office, *Kew:*
Corres. etc. 1852-1902 [MH 12/10645-57]; staff
reg. 1852-1921 [MH 9/1].

Andover [5] (partly in Wilts.).
See Ian Anstruther, *The Scandal of the Andover
Workhouse* (1973).
Hampshire Record Office, Winchester:
B. Min's 1835-1930; ledgers 1835-1930; other ac's
1855-1919; letter books 1846-1930; corres. 1837-
78; papers relating to the Andover W'h. scandal
1845-6; porter's book 1889-90; vouchers 1870-78;
provisions tenders book 1911-31.
Public Record Office, Kew:
Corres. etc. 1837-41, 1881-1900 [MH 12/10661-
66]; staff reg. 1837-1921 [MH 9/1].

Ash (Incorporation, to 1846) (Long Sutton).
See under Surrey.

Basingstoke [7] (partly in Berks.).
Hampshire Record Office, Winchester:
B. Min's 1835-1930; c'tee min's 1910-36; ledger
1923-30; SAC min's 1877-1903.
Public Record Office, Kew:
Corres. etc. 1834-1900 [MH 12/10669-98]; staff
reg. 1837-1921 [MH 9/2].

Bournemouth and Christchurch (1835-1900) see
Christchurch.
Bournemouth was a separate PLU from 1900.

Bradfield [4] (Mortimer West End).
See under Berkshire.

Catherington [24].
Hampshire Record Office, Winchester:
B. Min's 1900-29; ledger 1918-21; Assessment
C'tee min's 1886-1926.
Public Record Office, Kew:
Corres. etc. 1834-1900 [MH 12/10701-09]; staff
reg. 1837-1921 [MH 9/4].

Christchurch (pre-1837).
Dorset Record Office, Dorchester (most items
also on microfilm at **Lansdowne Library,**
Bournemouth):
A. Overseers of poor ac's (incl. rate assessments
and lists of allowances to poor, by tithing) 1728-
1836; appr's (and to whom bound) 1699-1744; poor
rates 1775-1836; reg. of inmates 1812-35; weekly
returns of inmates' employment 1768-1834.
B. Min's 1824-5; relief book 1821-35; ac's 1800-35;
clothing returns 1764-1805; provisions: returns
1768-1809, ledger 1805-07, ac's 1822-35.
See also **Holdenhurst**, below.

Christchurch [17] (**Bournemouth and
Christchurch** 1835-1900; from 1900 **Bournemouth**
was a separate PLU).
Dorset Record Office, Dorchester (most items
also on microfilm at **Lansdowne Library,**
Bournemouth):

B. Min's 1835-47, 1852-66, 876-87, 1892-1930
(incl c'tees 1923-30); C'tee min's: SAC 1877-1902,
Assessment 1899-1921, Finance 1900-33, W'h.
Visiting 1912-20, Cottage Home Visiting 1908-29,
sub-c'tees 1925-29; staff service reg's 1897-1948;
w'h. day books 1834-43.
Public Record Office, Kew:
Corres. etc. 1835-1900 [MH 12/10710-37]; staff
reg. 1837-1921 [MH 9/5].

Droxford [22].
Hampshire Record Office, Winchester:
B. Min's 1835-1930; ledgers 1836-1928; parochial
ledgers 1848-1927; letter books 1835-39, 1843-45;
Assessment C'tee min's 1862-66.
Public Record Office, Kew:
Corres. etc. 1834-1900 [MH 12/10751-66]; staff
reg. 1837-1921 [MH 9/6].

Fareham [21].
Hampshire Record Office, Winchester:
A. Births reg. 1914-30; deaths reg. 1914-43;
casuals adm. and discharge book 1924-25; vac.
reg's 1879-1929; settlement exam. book 1843-47.
B. Min's 1835-1930; c'tee min's 1903-25; ledgers
1825-1916; Assessment C'tee min's 1925-27;
master's journals 1929-48; visitors' book 1924-33;
garden and pig ac's 1891-1949; inventory book
1914-47.
Public Record Office, Kew:
Corres. etc. 1834-36, 1840-50, 1855-1900 [MH
12/10767-86]; staff reg. 1837-1921 [MH 9/7].

Farnborough [28] (Incorporation: 1794-1869).
Hampshire Record Office, Winchester:
B. Min's 1837-57; ac's 1794-1828.
Public Record Office, Kew:
Corres. etc. 1846-1870 [MH 12/10790-91]; staff
reg. 1837-69 [MH 9/7].

Farnham [28] (Aldershot, Dockenfield).
See under Surrey (and also **Alton**, above).

Fordingbridge [15] (partly in Wilts.).
Hampshire Record Office, Winchester:
B. Min's 1835-1919; ledgers 1914-18; Assessment
C'tee min's 1889-1909; SAC min's 1877-1903.
Public Record Office, Kew:
Corres. etc. 1839-1900 [MH 12/10792-803]; staff
reg. 1837-1921 [MH 9/7].

Forest, New see under **New Forest**.

Hartley Wintney [8].
Hampshire Record Office, Winchester:
A. Indoor relief books 1850-51, 1858-94; medical
relief books 1849-86 (gaps).
B. Master's day book 1869-73; clothing and
provisions ac's 1849-96; inventory books 1852-55,
1873-75.
Public Record Office, Kew:
Corres. etc. 1834- Jul. 1871, 1874-1900 [MH 12/
10804-19]; staff reg. 1837-1921 [MH 9/8].
See also under **Alton**.

Hampshire *continued*

Havant [26].
Hampshire Record Office, Winchester:
B. Min's 1856-1930.
Portsmouth City Records Office:
B. Assessment C'tee min's 1916-27.
Public Record Office, Kew:
Corres. etc. 1834-42, 1857-79, 1883-1900 [MH 12/10820-44]; staff reg. 1837-1921 [MH 9/8].

Headley [29] (Incorporation to 1869; absorbed by **Alton** and **Petersfield** PLUs).
Public Record Office, Kew:
Staff reg. 1852-67 [MH 9/8]; no MH 12 records.

Holdenhurst (later **Christchurch** PLU).
Dorset Record Office, Dorchester:
B. Overseers of poor ac's 1830-38.

Hungerford [1] (Coombe).
See under Berkshire.

Hursley [14].
No locally held records known.
Public Record Office, Kew:
Corres. etc. 1835-1900 [MH 12/10845-52]; staff reg. 1837-1921 [MH 9/9].

Isle of Wight see **Wight, Isle of.**

Kingsclere [2].
Hampshire Record Office, Winchester:
A. Adm. and discharge books 1874-79, 1907-50; indoor relief lists and abstracts 1837-1930; births reg's 1866-1930; deaths reg's 1866-1956; creed reg. 1902-14; punishment books 1871-1936; inmates' property reg's 1914-49; MO's report and exam. books 1914-53; reg. of boarded-out children 1910-40; DMO's relief book 1872-76; census reg. of children 1873-1900.
B. Min's 1835-1930; C'tee min's: House and boarding-out 1910-37, Assessment 1862-1926; master's journals and reports 1922-30; pauper description book 1835-37; chaplain's report books 1914-53; visitors' books (lunatics) 1912-48; ac's 1910-51.
Public Record Office, Kew:
Corres. etc. 1838-1900 [MH 12/10853-64]; staff reg. 1837-1921 [MH 9/9].

Lymington [19].
Hampshire Record Office, Winchester:
A. Creed reg's 1924-51; punishment books 1914-45.
B. Ledger 1914-16; chaplain's report book 1926-51.
Public Record Office, Kew:
Corres. etc. 1834-1900 [MH 12/10865-82]; staff reg. 1837-1921 [MH 9/10].

Midhurst [27] (South Ambersham, until 1844).
See under Sussex.

Newbury [3] (Newtown).
See under Berkshire.

New Forest [18] (partly in Wilts.).
Hampshire Record Office, Winchester:
B. Min's 1848-1930; ledgers 1847-48, 1871-73, 1923-30; parochial ledger 1915-20.
Public Record Office, Kew:
Corres. etc. 1862 - Jul. 1871, 1875-1900 [MH 12/10885-95]; staff reg. 1837-1921 [MH 9/12].

Petersfield [23].
Hampshire Record Office, Winchester:
B. Boarding-out C'tee min's 1910-40; parochial ledgers 1897-1927.
Public Record Office, Kew:
Corres. etc. 1834-1900 [MH 12/10896-913]; staff reg. 1837-1921 [MH 9/13].

Portsea/Portsmouth [25] (from 1836).
Portsmouth City Records Office:
Records of the Portsmouth w'h. administered by parish overseers from c.1737 on are also held.
A. *Lunacy:* lunatic lists 1867-1929, reg. of patients in City Mental Hospital 1896-1939, Asylum charges for pauper patients 1899-1917, mental defectives in Infirmary 1921-28; *Settlement:* removal expenses ac's 1925-34; *Welfare of women and children:* reg's of children under control of Guardians 1901-47, appr. indentures and adoption ag'mts 1899-1930, reg's: appr's 1926-46, servants 1924-49, those sent to Homes and Training Institutions 1897-1949, children boarded-out 1928-49, visits to servants 1903-31, claims made on other authorities for maintenance of children 1923-27; emigration of children 1894-1911; *Guardians' finance:* collector's receipt and exp. 1889-1928, exp. for dependents in
B. Min's 1838-1930; resolutions 1895-1921; agendas 1905-32; C'tee min's: Removal 1871-73, Infirmary 1898-1935, Children's Home 1901-48, Ladies' 1901-30, W'h. 1906-48, Buildings and Farm 1908-48, Contract and Workshops 1909-34, Boarding-out 1910-48; in-letters 1851-1929; out-letters to LGB and MoH 1879-1926; out-letters: general 1870-1920, removals 1880-88, financial 1919-26, misc. 1913; ledgers 1860-1928; finance books 1884-1931; treasurer's ledgers 1906-31; parochial ledger 1848-62; non-settled poor ac's 1899-1948; Guardians' statutory financial statements 1879-1930; annual lunatic claim 1911-15; *Staff:* service reg's 1861-1948, reg. of appointments 1861-99, National Insurance stamp books 1912-29, contracts and bonds 1895-1927, wage negotiations 1889-1952; misc. non-PL maps 1902-46; non-resident poor out relief 1912-48; *Stat's:* weekly returns (form A) 1911-12, Pauperism (form B) 1904-30, pauper classification book 1890-96; *Administration:* buildings 1879-1938, central authority 1868-1932, medical 1893-1937, general 1906-42, newspaper cuttings 1927-58; collector's ledgers 1928-36; overseers' and collectors' summary ac's 1836-1927; collectors' misc. 1870-1962; treasurer's ac's 1888-1930; loans book 1879-1933; security bonds for loans 1881-1930; *Relieving officer:* receipt and exp. 1912-31, quarterly returns

ledger 1900-18, outdoor relief statements 1912-27, pay sheets 1928-29; *W'h.*: petty cash books 1885-1929, chaplain's reports 1899-1949, inventory book 1929-52, w'h. school reg'ns 1906, survey of Institution at Milton 1904; *W'h. plans:* paupers' (unadopted schemes) mid-C19, aged couples 1888, children's 1838-1932, common rooms, offices and workshops 1844-1935, proposed sanatorium early C20, fire escapes and verandas 1902, water drainage 1904-5; *W'h. Infirmary (now St. Mary's Hospital):* administration 1898-1919, chapel service reg's 1899-1946, chaplain's reports 1929-44, clerk of works notebooks 1902-09, extensions to W'h. Infirmary papers 1910-19, photos. 1898-1937, *plans:* site 1904-49, extensions 1907-11, drainage etc. 1913; *description:* Phthisical (sic) patients building 1911-14, nurses' home 1900-26, MO's residence 1908; *Children's Home Cosham:* construction papers and plans 1926, chaplain's reports 1929-39; *Assessment C'tee min's:* Portsmouth 1880-1940, Alverstoke 1912-27; mental health 1914-64.
Public Record Office, Kew:
Corres. etc. 1834-1900 [MH 12/10916-63]; staff reg. 1837-1921 [MH 9/13].

Ringwood [16].
Hampshire Record Office, Winchester:
B. Min's 1835-1930.
Public Record Office, Kew:
Corres. etc. 1834-1900 [MH 12/10971-82]; staff reg. 1837-1921 [MH 9/14].

Romsey [13] (partly in Wilts.).
Hampshire Record Office, Winchester:
A. Births reg. 1925-31; deaths reg. 1835-1925.
B. Min's 1851-55, 1858-63; Boarding-out C'tee min's 1890-1934; ledger 1927-30.
Public Record Office, Kew:
Corres. etc. 1834-1900 [MH 12/10983-96]; staff reg. 1837-1921 [MH 9/14].

Southampton [30] (Incorporation 1772-1909; PLU from 1909).
Southampton City Records Office:
A. Valuation lists, various, between 1895 and 1921; rate books, various, between 1732 and 1917; settlement exam. reg's 1711-1901 (gaps, indexed to 1858); settlement of lunatics reg's (indexed) 1878-88, 1896-1923; settlement of bastards reg's (indexed) 1811-39; exam. and removal orders 1817-42, 1877-8; out relief books 1787-89 and n.d.; list of rate defaulters 1833-36; ag'mts re. paupers not in own Union 1870-73, 1917-28.
B. Min's 1818-1930; C'tee min's: New Poor House 1847, Poor Law Amendment Bill 1856, W'h. 1878-1920, Infirmary 1904-30, Distress 1905-10, others 1882-1930; parochial ledgers 1909-25; visitors' books 1779-1833, 1866-1914 (lunatics 1888-90, 1899-1900); reports on inmates 1900; list of unrated tenements 1821; city survey 1838; county rate papers 1775-93; abstract of Guardians' ac's 1775-

1868; printed ac's and abstracts 1851-1929 (gaps); byelaws for poor 1817-8; building bills 1819-23; sale of land 1829-31; PLC papers 1834; various Parliamentary papers re. Southampton 1772-1856; PLB, LGB orders 1850-1909; PLC reports 1817, 1834-5; PL returns 1787, 1822; incorporation records, 1906-08, 1923, and maps 1895, 1923; chairman's agenda book 1922-30; Southampton overseers' min's 1919-26 and overseers' receipts and exp. 1918-24; non-settled poor ac's 1862-72; reg. of mortgages and securities 1864-1922; Guardians' report 1850; weekly returns 1882-87; report on inmates c.1900; returns of outdoor relief arrangements 1904, 1921, 1924 (medical 1909, 1924); letter books 1832-1911, 1920-43; legal proceedings against Guardians 1791-1805; proposed rules for school of industry c.1850; employees bonds etc. 1865-1920; papers re. Russian emigrants 1879-80; papers re. emigration of children to Canada 1902-07; ag'mt re pauper lunatics 1890-1912; notes re. w'h. incident 1906; ag'mts for employment and food 1780, 1810; MO contract 1926; schoolmaster dispute papers 1892; plans of w'h. etc. 1848-1910; visitors' books 1779-1833, 1909-14 (lunatics 1888-90, 1899-1900).
Southampton City Records Office also has a large collection of parish and charity relief papers.
Public Record Office, Kew:
Corres. etc. 1834 - July 1871, 1873-1900 [MH 12/10997-11025]; staff reg. 1837-1921 [MH 9/15].

South Stoneham [20].
Southampton City Records Office:
A. Lists of indoor poor 1832, 1838, 1855-57.
B. Min's 1839-1930 (gaps); C'tee min's: House 1906-08, 1916-25, Farm 1903-25; ledgers 1895-1925 (gaps); treasurer's ledger 1912-15; half yearly abstracts 1903-07; mortgage papers 1911, 1930; appointment of Guardians 1902, 1922; abstract of ac's 1904.
Public Record Office, Kew:
Corres. etc. 1834-1900 [MH 12/11035-56]; staff reg. 1837-1921 [MH 9/15].

Stockbridge [9] (partly in Wilts.).
Hampshire Record Office, Winchester:
A. Deaths reg. 1914-39; reg. of boarded-out children 1926-28.
B. Min's 1835-1922 (gaps); boarding-out records 1920-30; inventory book 1915-22; ac's from 1921.
Public Record Office, Kew:
Corres. etc. 1834-1900 [MH 12/11063-73]; staff reg. 1837-1921 [MH 9/16].

Stoneham, South see under South Stoneham.

Whitchurch [6].
Hampshire Record Office, Winchester:
B. Min's 1835-1930; Assessment C'tee min's 1862-1923.
Public Record Office, Kew:
Corres. etc. 1834-88, 1897-1900 [MH 12/11074-83]; staff reg. 1837-1921 [MH 9/18].

Hampshire continued

Wight, Isle of [32] (Incorporation 1770-1865; PLU from 1865).
Isle of Wight County Record Office, Newport:
A. W'h. weekly min's and outdoor relief lists 1778-1930; lists of inmates 1790-1813, 1820-39; descriptions of paupers 1834; reg. of w'h. appr's 1802-33; bastardy deposits 1781-95.
B. W'h.: quarterly min's 1788-1836, ledger book 1836-1930, parochial ledger 1867-1923; treasurer's ledger ac's 1866-1930, non-resident and non-settled poor ac's 1908-15, letter books 1892-1933; inventory 1910-31; Assessment C'tee min's 1865-1905; LGB orders 1844-87; Works C'tee min's 1869-96; weekly provisions 1823-31; quarterly bills 1784-1800.
Public Record Office, Kew:
Corres. etc. 1834-1899 [MH 12/11084-144]; staff reg. 1837-1921 [MH 9/19].

Wimborne (Hampreston).
See under Dorset.

Winchester (New) [10].
Hampshire Record Office, Winchester:
A. Adm. and discharge books 1835-1951 (gaps); births reg's 1835-1931; deaths reg's 1835-1938; creed reg's 1925-46; punishment book 1914-38.
B. Min's 1835-46, 1891-1925; C'tee min's: Assessment 1893-1914, SAC 1899-1903; master's journals 1901-40; MO's reports etc. 1880-1911; visitors' books (lunatics) 1895-1925; ac's 1896-1950.
Public Record Office, Kew:
Corres. etc. 1838-1900 [MH 12/11168-90]; staff reg. 1837-1921 [MH 9/19].

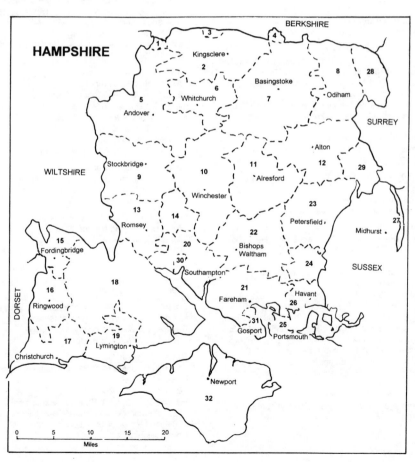

HEREFORDSHIRE

· Except when shown otherwise, records are at *Hereford and Worcester Record Office (Hereford Branch), Hereford.*

Abergavenny (Fwthog).
See under Wales: Monmouthshire.

Bromyard [9] (partly Worcs.).
A. Adm. and discharge books 1840-1929; casual (vagrants) adm. book 1911-2, 1925-31; porter's adm. and discharge books 1900-16; valuation lists (various).
B. Min's 1836-1930; C'tee min's: Finance 1880-1930, House 1915-21, 1927-30, Visiting 1911-15, Boarding-out 1911-29, RSA (rough) 1872-84, 1893-96, Assessment 1899-1927; reg. of appointments 1879-1930; ac's ledger 1912-21.
Public Record Office, Kew:
Corres. etc. 1834-1900 [MH 12/4285-306]; staff reg. 1837-1921 [MH 9/3].

Cleobury Mortimer [6] (Farley).
See under Shropshire.

Dore [11] (partly in Monmouths.).
A. Births reg. 1914-30; indoor relief lists 1854-1925 (gaps); adm. and discharge books 1850-1916 (gaps) (casuals 1876-1923); case papers c.1907-29; valuation lists (various).
B. Min's 1837-1930; financial statements 1900-04; SAC min's 1897-1909; PLC orders forming PLU 1837.
Public Record Office, Kew:
Corres. etc. 1834-1900 [MH 12/4308-22]; staff reg. 1837-1921 [MH 9/6].

Hay [10] (Bredwardine, Clifford, Cusop, Dorstone, Whitney).
A. Valuation lists (various).
Otherwise see under Wales: Brecknock.

Hereford [12].
See Sylvia A. Morrell, 'The Poor Law in Hereford, 1836-1851', *Woolhope Naturalists Field Club* **41** (1974/5).
A. Reg. of non-resident poor 1909-10; valuation lists (various) 1910-28.
B. Min's 1836-1930; C'tee min's: Finance 1919-30, House 1914-23, 1928-30, Children's Homes 1910-30, RSA 1873-88, Assessment 1862-1900, 1910-19; PLC orders forming PLU 1836-7; statement of ac's 1928; LGB letter books 1878-9, 1893-95; meetings agendas 1906-10; financial statements 1900-04, 1928; Assessment C'tee appeals 1905-12; corres. etc. of Superintendent Registrar 1836-42; portrait of Board members c.1890/1900.
Public Record Office, Kew:
Corres. etc. 1839-76, 1889-1900 [MH 12/4323-45]; staff reg. 1837-1921 [MH 9/8].

Kington [7] (partly Radnors.).
A. Creed reg. 1905-12; indoor relief lists 1915-29; adm. and discharge books 1906-27 (casuals 1917-30); valuation lists (various).
B. Min's 1836-1930; treasurer's ledger 1924-29; Assessment C'tee min's 1862-1923; vac. officer's notices and report book 1888-1935.
Public Record Office, Kew:
Corres. etc. 1834-82, 1893-1900 [MH 12/4348-62]; staff reg. 1837-1921 [MH 9/9].

Knighton [1] (Adforton, Brampton Bryan, Buckton and Coxall, Letton and Newton, Walford).
See under Wales: Radnorshire.

Ledbury [13] (partly Worcs.).
A. Appr. indentures 1848-85; marriage notice books 1842-1912.
B. Min's 1836-1930; Ladies Visiting C'tee min's 1895-1926; letter book 1851-58; w'h. deeds etc. 1836-87; corres. etc. 1850-1905; treasurer's ledgers 1919-23; postage book 1923-26; RSA min's 1872-80; Assessment C'tee min's 1862-1927.
Public Record Office, Kew:
Corres. etc. 1839-1900 [MH 12/4364-82]; staff reg. 1837-1921 [MH 9/10].

Leominster [4].
A. Valuation lists (various).
B. Min's 1852-1930 (gaps); Boarding-out C'tee min's 1911-21; w'h. deeds, plans etc. 1836-41; Assessment C'tee min's 1887-1927.
Public Record Office, Kew:
Corres. etc. 1834-82, 1886-1900 [MH 12/4385-403]; staff reg. 1837-1921 [MH 9/10].

Ludlow [2] (Aston, Burrington, Downton, Elton, Leinthall Starkes, Leintwardine (and North Side), Ludford, Richards Castle, Wigmore).
See under Shropshire.

Monmouth [14] (Ganarew, Faraway, Llanrothal, Welsh Bicknor and Newton, Whitchurch).
A. Valuation lists (various).
Otherwise see under Wales: Monmouthshire.

Newent [16] (Aston Ingham, Linton, Walford, 1835-6 only).
See under Gloucestershire.

Presteigne [3] (Byton, Combe, Lower and Upper Kinsham, Knill, Lingen, Ross, Nash and Little Brampton, Stapleton, Willey, 1836 only).
See under Wales: Brecknock.

Ross [15] (partly Glos.).
A. Relief order books 1915-24; valuation lists (various).
B. Min's 1836-1930; C'tee min's: Finance 1905-30, House 1905-22, RSA 1872-85, Assessment 1899-1927 (chairman's min. book 1908-27); letter books 1904-19, 1921-28; Public Loans Works Commissioner's ac's 1905-6.

Gloucestershire Record Office, *Gloucester.*
A. Poor rates for Ruardean, and for Linton and Upton Bishop (Herefs.) 1914-25.
Public Record Office, Kew:
Corres. etc. 1834-56, 1860-79, 1881-1900 [MH 12/ 4405-25]; staff reg. 1837-1921 [MH 9/14].

Tenbury [5] (Brimfield, Lit. Hereford, Stoke Bliss).
A. Valuation lists (Little Hereford and Brimfield only).
Otherwise see under Worcestershire.

Weobley [8].
B. Min's 1834-90 (gaps); RSA min's 1891-99.
Public Record Office, Kew:
Corres. etc. 1834-1898 [MH 12/4428-40]; staff reg. 1837-1921 [MH 9/18].

HEREFORDSHIRE

OXFORDSHIRE

The PLU in which each parish lay is shown in C.G. Harris, *Oxfordshire Parish Registers and Bishops Transcripts,* (Oxfordshire F.H.S., 4th edition, 1993).

Unless shown otherwise, records are at **Oxfordshire Archives,** *Oxford.*
Records under 75 years old (from last date) are normally closed to the public.
Note. In addition to the following, there are a number of assessments, valuation lists, receipt books etc. relating to rate collection, removal orders 1838-72, and lists of persons wishing to emigrate 1845.

Abingdon [9] (Marsh and Toot Baldon, Binsey, Burcott, Chislehampton, Clifton Hampden, Culham, Drayton St. Leonard, Nuneham Courtenay, Sandford on Thames, Seacourt, Stadhampton).
See under Berkshire.

Banbury [1] (partly in Glos., Northants., Warw.).
See J.S.W. Gibson, 'Sponsored emigration of paupers from Banbury Poor Law Union, 1834-60', *Oxon. FH* **2.**7, 1982 (based on P.R.O. MH 12).
A. Medical cert's to detain paupers 1888-90.
B. Min's 1839-1930 (chairman's 1916-30); C'tee min's: House 1904-20, Institution 1920-30, Boarding-out 1910-30, Special 1909-29, Children's Home 1914-30.
Public Record Office, Kew:
Corres. etc. 1834-1896 [MH 12/9577-610]; staff reg. 1837-1921 [MH 9/2].

Bicester [4] (partly in Bucks.).
See W. Wing, *Brief annals of the Bicester PLU and its component parishes,* various editions, 1877-81.
A. Notices of death and discharge of pauper lunatics (Littlemore) 1857-92; annual returns of pauper lunatics 1842-62; adm. and discharge book 1834-36; appl. and report book (Bicester 1837, Bletchington 1838-1920); outdoor relief lists, various between 1838 and 1909; relieving officer's receipt and exp. books, various, between 1840 and 1868; requests for medical attention in Bletchington 1876-78; reports on children boarded-out 1894-5; medical cert's: cause of death (Bletchington) 1870-1905; vac. reg's, various, 1853-98; annual lists of children over 5 in schools 1877-79; census of children under 14 (Bletchington) 1877; school fees appl. and report book (Bletchington) 1877-90; school attendance cards 1884; deaths in w'h. 1886.
B. Min's 1835-1928; letter books 1844-62, 1879-88; lists of Guardians etc. 1874-95; abstracts of poor relief etc. 1839-47; county precepts (Oxon. 1845-84, Bucks. 1846-69); parish precepts 1873-92; financial statements 1868-84; overseers' receipts and exp. 1839-84; PLC, PLB and LGB orders and corres. 1836-71; general corres. 1836-1911; tenders etc. 1836-71; Visiting C'tee report book 1840-55; w'h. ac's book 1837-39; Bletchington relieving officer's weekly ac's books 1875-89; orders to retailers for supplies 1891-1906; non-settled poor relief ac's

Oxfordshire: **Bicester** *continued*

1845-48; DMO weekly returns 1836, 1846, 1892; collector's ac's book 1881-1920; registrar's quarterly ac's 1838-65; 1871 census plans; weekly vac. returns 1848 (sic); abstracts of valuation lists 1869-81; weekly reports of inspector of nuisances and notices to owners of premises 1873; canal boat inspections 1889-1921; school exam. schedules 1878-86; school attendance officer's report books (Bletchington 1877-1902, Deddington 1909-16).
   Public Record Office, Kew:
   Corres. etc. 1834-1900 [MH 12/9614-34]; staff reg. 1837-1921 [MH 9/2].

Brackley [5] (Finmere, Mixbury).
See under Northamptonshire.

Bradfield [12] (Goring, Mapledurham, Whitchurch).
See under Berkshire.

Buckingham [6] (Lillingstone Lovell, Boycott (Stowe), to 1844).
See under Buckinghamshire.

Chipping Norton [2] (partly in Glos., Warw.).
Asterisked records not open to the public for 75 years.
   A. Adm. and discharge books 1906-16, *1919-52 (vagrants *1926-7); notice of births for purpose of registration *1920-29; notice to coroner of deaths of lunatics 1902-18; punishment book *1914-36; reg. of friends and relatives of inmates *1906-53; inventory of property of deceased inmates *1922-48; MO's exam. of children *1914-32, inmates *1914-43, casuals *1929-39; medical journals *1928-9; porters' visitors' books *1921, *1925.
   B. Min's 1837-1927 (gaps); C'tee min's: Assessment 1862-1904, SAC 1902-3, W'h. *1928-9; reg. of securities 1904-30; w'h. spec. 1836; ledgers 1840-1 (incl. individual parishes), 1894-99; parochial ledgers 1881-84, 1902-04; returns of infectious diseases, number of persons relieved 1911-14; sup'an. reg. *1903-30; special reports on casuals *1925-31; master's half yearly reports 1914-31; provision and consumption ac's: daily 1929-34, summary 1921-40; weekly provisions 1929-34; clothing ac's 1920-45;, necessaries ac's 1927-34; institution inventory 1919-38; MO's reports 1912-14; House or Institution C'tee report book 1919-47; Visiting C'tee for Lunatics report books 1921-41; chaplain's report book *1914-28; wages receipt book *1920-30; master's day books 1919-36 (summary 1920-31); receipts and exp. 1927-34; farm ac's 1921-37; oakum ac's 1906-38; quarry book 1925-27; barber's weekly shaves and haircuts 1919-45; relieving officer's outdoor relief receipts and exp.: Chipping Norton dist. 1913-16, Charlbury dist. 1926-31.
   Public Record Office, Kew:
   Corres. etc. 1834-1900 [MH 12/9637-54]; staff reg. 1837-1921 [MH 9/5].

Faringdon [7] (Little Faringdon, Grafton, Langford, Radcot).
See under Berkshire.

Headington [11] (partly in Bucks. until 1844).
See E. Mason, 'Headington Union', *Oxon. FH*, **5**,3, 1989.
   These records are part of Oxford City Archives. They can be seen at the Oxfordshire Archives searchroom, but prior notice is required.
   B. Min's 1841-1927 (missing 1902-4, 1917-19): these incl. lists of adm's and those receiving short term outdoor relief 1841-48, children about to leave Cowley School from 1879, appr. outside PLU from 1851, foster parents and children 1874, boys joining fleet and Grimsby from 1870s, many removals.
   Bodleian Library, Oxford.
   B. Printed ac's, listing Guardians and officers, 1888.
   Public Record Office, Kew:
   Corres. etc. 1834-1900 [MH 12/9658-78]; staff reg. 1837-1921 [MH 9/8].

Henley [16] (partly in Berks., Bucks.)
   B. Min's 1835-1928.
   Public Record Office, Kew:
   Corres. etc. 1834-1900 [MH 12/9681-701]; staff reg. 1837-1921 [MH 9/8].

Oxford (United parishes, 1771-1837).
   No original records survive, but see *V.C.H. Oxon.* **4**, pp. 346-50, for this and the subsequent PLU; and J.S.W. Gibson, 'City of Oxford PLU Records', *Oxon. FH* **6**, 4 (1993), for a detailed description of the printed reports and ac's.
   Oxford Central Library, Centre for Oxfordshire Studies:
   A. Printed ac's (July-June) 1807/8, 1808/9, 1812/3, 1814/5, 1816-7, 1826-7, 1833/4, 1836-7 (microfilm, from Bodleian copies), with names of many tradesmen suppliers, places refunding relief of surnamed individuals, removals of named paupers and some places; from 1833/4 forenames as well as surnames given, individuals named in bastardy ac's, families maintained from out-parishes and paupers resident out of Oxford.
   Bodleian Library, Oxford.
   Printed ac's, as at Centre for Oxon. Studies above.

Oxford [10] (PLU from 1837).
   A. Baptisms reg. 1843-93 (transcript available, also at *Centre for Oxfordshire Studies* and *Society of Genealogists*).
   No other original records survive, see note above.
   Oxford Central Library, Centre for Oxforshire Studies:
   A. Printed ac's 1837-39, 1841-45, 1852/3, 1855-59, 1861/2, 1863-73 (on microfilm from Bodleian copies), 1874-1915 (missing 1884/5, 1886/7), 1919-30: incl. bastardy ac's 1837-45, out-parish papers 1837-45, deaths 1841-1930, children capable of going into service 1841-53, Guardians, staff (with salaries), lunatics 1869-1930, indoor and outdoor poor (incl. addresses) 1872-1915, children relieved in school 1872-1930, settlement cases and non-settled poor 1896-1930, service children and appr's 1897-1930, births c.1900-30.

Oxfordshire: **Oxford** *continued*

B. Printed ac's (various) as above; dietaries 1869-1930.
Bodleian Library, Oxford.
Printed ac's, as at Centre for Oxon. Studies above.
Public Record Office, Kew:
Corres. etc. 1834-1900 [MH 12/9706-27]; staff reg. 1837-1921 [MH 9/12].

Thame [13] (partly in Bucks.).
B. Min's 1835-1928; Assessment C'tee min's 1862-92; SAC min's 1893-1903; dietary 1836; overseer's min's 1896-1916.
Public Record Office, Kew:
Corres. etc. 1834-1900 [MH 12/9732-50]; staff reg. 1837-1921 [MH 9/17].

Wallingford [15] (Benson, Berrick Salome, Crowmarsh Gifford, Dorchester, Ewelme, Mongewell, Newington, Newnham Murren, North and South Stoke, Warborough).
See under Berkshire.

Witney [8] (partly in Berks., Glos. until 1844).
B. Min's 1835-1931 (gaps); Assessment C'tee min's 1862-98.
Public Record Office, Kew:
Corres. etc. 1834-1900 [MH 12/9753-71]; staff reg. 1837-1921 [MH 9/19].

Woodstock [3].
A. Baptisms reg. 1866-1948.
B. Min's 1835-1931; C'tee min's: Assessment 1862-1926, Boarding-out 1921-30, SAC 1898-1903, Visiting (lunatics) 1909-40; MO's report book 1914-54; service reg. 1906-30; financial statements 1835-6; precept to Steeple Aston 1898-1903; extract of ac's 1840; cuttings scrapbook from 1877.
Public Record Office, Kew:
Corres. etc. 1834-1900 (missing 1847-50) [MH 12/9775-92]; staff reg. 1837-1921 [MH 9/19].

Wycombe [14] (Chinnor, Ibstone, Lewknor Uphill, Stokenchurch).
See under Buckinghamshire.

See also J.S.W. Gibson, 'Transported convicts' families in North Oxon., 1846' (Banbury, Bicester, Chipping Norton, Witney, Woodstock PLUs), *Oxon. FH* **2**.7, 1982; and 'Pauper emigration' (Bicester, Chipping Norton and Witney PLUs), *Oxon. FH* **2**.8, 1982.

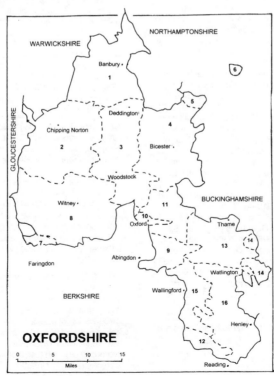

SHROPSHIRE

See V.J. Walsh, 'Old and New Poor Laws in Shropshire 1820-1870', *Midland History* 2 (1973/4).

Unless shown otherwise, records are at *Shropshire Record Office, Shrewsbury.*
They are (at least partially) listed in *A Guide to the Shropshire Records*, 1952, pp. 31-41. All records are closed for thirty years, though some post-1930 will be closed for up to 100 years.

Atcham (Incorporation).
  A. Reg. of appr's 1802-06, 1812-14; adm's 1794-1836; removal orders to and from Pontesbury (1698-1829) and Minsterley (1771-1831).
  B. Order books 1792-1801, 1831-36; journal 1832-38; ledgers (ac's with various firms) 1832-38; mortgages 1792-1843; abstract of ac's (for late Incorporation) 1845.

Atcham (PLU) [7] (partly Montgomerys.).
  Amalgamated with Shrewsbury in the 1870s and later known as **Atcham and Shrewsbury**. For records of all periods the **Shrewsbury** entry should also be consulted.
  A. Removal orders from the Union 1865-66 and evidence in removal cases 1870-75; creed register (Shrewsbury only) 1906-14; outdoor relief appl. report books: Atcham 1864-71, Ford 1862-72, Shrewsbury 1871-75; lists 1848-73; vagrant out-relief lists: Ford 1868-70, Shrewsbury 1871-2; indoor relief lists of foreign paupers 1919-22; rate books (Alberbury, Cardiston, Ford, Habberley, Pontesbury, Minsterley) 1837-64 (gaps); SAC school fees appl. and report book 1877-83.
  B. Min's 1836-1930; C'tee min's: Children's 1918-30, Ladies 1908-11, Berrington Hospital 1926-30, RSA 1875-87; ledgers (incl. parochial) 1836-1930 (missing 1855, 1879), petty cash 1911-16, 1928-47; financial statements 1849-67, 1890-1920; half yearly estimates 1916-30; salaries books 1912-23; weekly returns (form A) 1839-68 (gaps); appl. report book (abstract) 1837-39; relief order books (under parishes) 1839-94 (see also Shrewsbury); pauper classification books 1850-79, 1882-91; medical appl's 1842-64; letter books 1837-1924; w'h. medical relief form 1871-74; day books (for receiving house, 143 Abbey Foregate) 1919-46; daily provision consumption ac's 1874-5; list of Guardians 1838-43; poll book for election of Guardians (St. Chad, St. Julian, St. Mary) 1871; Relieving Officer: appl. and report books, outdoor relief: Atcham 1837-8, Ford 1837; weekly outdoor relief: Atcham and Ford 1837-48, Condover 1837-40; receipt and exp. books 1848-59, ac's 1859-70; DMO returns (Ford and Shrewsbury) 1874-77; RSA: ledgers 1873-96, letter books 1873-95.
  Public Record Office, Kew:
  Corres. etc. 1834-1900 [MH 12/9822-46]; staff reg. 1837-1921 [MH 9/1].

Bridgnorth [17].
  A. Reg. of boarding-out children 1910-35; appr. indentures etc. 1847-87; removal orders 1901-19; creed reg's. 1884-1931.
  B. Min's 1859-64, 1884-1930; attendance book 1907-41; ledgers 1864-68, 1875-77, 1890-1930; letter books 1887-1927 (missing 1894); treasurer's book 1925-30; visitors' book 1928-48; Assessment C'tee min's 1887-1908; SAC min's 1889-90.
  Public Record Office, Kew:
  Corres. etc. 1834-1900 [MH 12/9850-68; staff reg. 1837-1921 [MH 9/3].

Bromsgrove [6] (Hunnington, Romsley).
See under Worcestershire.

Bromwich, West [4] (Oldbury, Warley).
See under Staffordshire.

Church Stretton [11].
  A. Adm. and discharge reg. 1918-26; births reg. 1843-55; out-relief order books 1890-1924; rate book: Shipton 1924; valuation lists (various places) 1904-16, 1924.
  B. Min's 1836-1930; Ladies Visiting C'tee min's 1893-1939; ledgers 1836-40, 1846-1930 (incl. parochial and non-settled poor 1853-70); parochial ledgers 1840-46, 1870-1907; treasurer's books 1889-97, 1920-23, and ac's 1926-30; master's report books 1915-22; Visiting c'tee: lunatics 1907-19; provisions ac's, dietaries etc. 1919-30; relieving officer's receipts and exp. ac's 1900-03; DMO relief book 1909-13; rate collectors' books: Acton Scott 1919-27, Shipton 1916-27, Wistanstow 1926-7; Assessment C'tee min's 1862-84; RSA: min's 1879-97, ledgers 1873-1908, parochial ledgers 1881-1906, treasurer's book 1873-78.
  Public Record Office, Kew:
  Corres. etc. 1834-1900 [MH 12/9869-81]; staff reg. 1837-1921 [MH 9/5].

Cleobury Mortimer [19] (partly Worcs., Heref.).
  A. Appr. papers 1828-37; removal orders 1839-45; pauper lists at formation of Union 1836; exam's 1836-39; inquest depositions (6) 1838-97; adm's to Salop Infirmary 1836-81; annual return of lunatics 1844; outdoor relief books 1836-41.
  B. Min's 1836-1930; ledgers 1836-1930; parochial ledgers 1864-78, 1890-1901; petty cash book 1925-41; letter books 1836-48, 1919-24; vac. papers 1841-60; Assessment C'tee min's 1862-94.
  Public Record Office, Kew:
  Corres. etc. 1843-1900 [MH 12/9882-95]; staff reg. 1837-1921 [MH 9/5].

Clun [10] (partly Montgomerys.).
  A. Pauper children discharged to service 1886-87; exam's and removals 1833-76; births reg. 1866-1939; deaths reg. 1866-1951; relief order books 1909-26; list of paupers relieved 1914 (printed); creed reg's c.1914-30; reg. of inmates c.1928-45; vac. reg's: Clun 1899-1916, Lydbury 1888-1911, Norbury 1891-1903; reg. of infants 1909-28 (and persons receiving infants 1907-29); relief of children:

appl. and report book 1912-19; Assessment C'tee: poor rate books: Clun 1882, Hillend 1871-82.

B. Min's 1844-1927; C'tee min's: House 1914-16, Boarding-out 1912-27, RSA 1872-96, SAC 1877-91; Guardians' declarations 1891-1928: list of Guardians 1887-8, 1914-5; attendance book 1908-11; ledgers 1858-61, 1867-70, 1875-1929; parochial ledgers 1861-1927; treasurer's ledgers ac's 1914-30; petty cash book 1887-1930; financial statement and loan ac's 1879-1929, half-yearly 1854-89; non-settled poor ac's 1916-29; fortnightly returns (form A) 1917-30, weekly returns 1907-14, 1924-30; various plans and spec's 1840-1927; relief of children: receipts and exp. 1915-28, Boarding-out C'tee letter book 1914-27; misc. corres. 1841-89, 1910-30; treasurer's receipts and exp. 1873-1930; DMO relief books 1890-1925; Assessment C'tee: min's 1862-69, 1881-96, letter books 1877-1933 (and corres. re. valuations from 1835); RSA: ledgers 1873-1902, annual reports 1879-84, letter books 1872-86; SAC returns 1876-78, letter book 1877-83.

Public Record Office, Kew: Corres. etc. 1834-1900 [MH 12/9896-915]; staff reg. 1837-1921 [MH 9/5].

Drayton see Market Drayton.

Ellesmere (Incorporation, 1791).
B. Record of nos. of paupers in poor house: 1795, 1810, 1824.

Ellesmere [1] (PLU) (partly Flints.).
A. Births and deaths reg. 1866-1930.
B. Min's 1871-75, 1908-23; ledger 1928-30; treasurer's ac's 1921-30; staff reg's 1898-1930; Assessment C'tee min's 1897-1924; RSA min's 1893-4, (RDC) 1895-98.

Public Record Office, Kew: Corres. etc. 1834-1900 [MH 12/9935-50]; staff reg. 1837-1921 [MH 9/6].

Kidderminster [20] (Dowles).
See under Worcestershire.

Knighton [15] (Bedstone, Bettwys y Crwyn, Bucknell, Llanfair Waterdine, Stowe).
See under Wales: Radnorshire.

Ludlow [16] (partly Herefs.).
A. Settlement, removal etc. c.1846, c.1857; adm. and discharge reg's 1846-81, 1890-94, 1900-08, 1911-13 (also school 1847-89, vagrants 1868-1947 (gaps)); school attendance books 1857-59, 1864-65, 1868-71, 1876-78; reg. of children boarded-out 1908-36; w'h. school reg. 1887-89; births reg. 1836-1944; deaths reg. 1837-66; reg. of sickness and mortality 1840-47; creed reg's 1869-1906; punishment book 1842-1912; marriage notice books 1895-1928; reg. of young persons under 16 hired for w'h. 1908-33; relieving officer: appl. and report books 1836-1943; weekly outdoor relief lists: Bromfield 1842, 1870-1923, Ashford Bowler 1847, Diddlebury 1845, general 1840-53, 1858-62, 1865-69;

receipts and exp. 1836-1918 (various places, dist's, many gaps); vagrants outdoor relief lists 1868-74; misc. rate books and valuation lists, various places, C19.

B. Min's 1836-1930 (missing 1893-95); Boarding-out C'tee min's 1869-72; ledgers 1836-1930 (gaps); treasurer's ledger 1927-30; parochial ledgers 1842-1927 (gaps); relieving officer's weekly returns 1850-59; financial statements 1872-1925 (gaps); in-relief weekly returns (form A) 1874-1930 (gaps), (form B) 1909-11, 1926-28; pauper classification books 1859-95 (gaps); out-relief order books 1848-1930 (gaps); letter books 1838-42, 1861-1921 (gaps); treasurer's books 1836-44, 1867-72, 1888-97, 1902-06, 1924-29; indoor relief list 1855-86 (gaps), 1909-11, 1914-16; MO's exam's of lunatics 1921-30; w'h. medical relief books 1857-1910 (gaps); porter's books 1839-45 (gaps); chaplain's report books 1921-33; master's journal and reports 1842-1933 (gaps); nurses' reports 1908, 1912-3; visitors' report books 1842-50, 1860-63, 1880-87, 1895-1902; outside visitors' book 1838-86; Lunatics Visiting C'tee book 1881-1904; master's day books 1848-54, 1867-74, 1889-93, 1909-16, 1928-32, receipts and exp. 1890-1935; farm ac's 1875-97; firewood ac's 1912-39; inventories 1901-07, 1921-45; clothing reg's, materials etc. 1849-84, 1922-25; shoemaker's book and ac's 1857-60, 1864; provision consumption books and ac's 1852-1930 (various, many gaps); necessaries and misc. ac's 1868-1917 (gaps); medical weekly returns (out relief) 1841-55, 1871-81; collectors' receipts and exp. 1896-1921; weekly list (classified) of paupers relieved 1853-59; Assessment C'tee min's 1875-97; SAC min's 1886-1904, 1917-24.

Public Record Office, Kew: Corres. etc. 1834-1900 [MH 12/9954-76]; staff reg. 1837-1921 [MH 9/10].

Madeley [12].
A. Relief order books: Madeley 1848-1930 (gaps), Broseley 1844-65; relieving officer's appl. and report books 1836-48, 1924-30; rate book 1840, (Stirchley) 1925; valuation lists: Madeley 1864, Stirchley 1902.
B. Min's 1836-1930; ledgers 1911-13, 1919-30; treasurer's ac's 1924-30; financial statements 1915-22; salaries reg. 1901-20; letter books 1897-1927; treasurer's receipts and exp. 1910-30; MO's report book 1914-22; Assessment C'tee: min's 1862-70, parochial ac's 1862-77; RSA min's 1872-1930; SAC fees order book 1883-1929.

Public Record Office, Kew: Corres. etc. 1834-1900 [MH 12/9981-98]; staff reg. 1837-1921 [MH 9/11].

Market Drayton [3].
A. Settlement exam's, removals and lunatics' case papers 1891-1908; Assessment C'tee rate books: Drayton in Hales 1881-1920, Childs Ercoll 1914, Tyrley (Staffs.) 1920, 1923, Woore 1922, Mucclestone 1923, Moreton Say 1924, 1926, Sutton upon Tern 1925; valuation list, Stoke upon Tern 1926.

Shropshire: Market Drayton *continued*

B. Min's 1836-1930; ledgers 1836-1930; parochial, non-resident and non-settled poor ledgers 1845-1902; letter books 1903-19.
Public Record Office, Kew:
Corres. etc. 1834-1900 [MH 12/9918-32]; staff reg. 1837-1921 [MH 9/6].

Montgomery [24] (Brompton and Rhiston, Chirbury, Worthen).
See under Wales: Montgomeryshire.

Newport [9] (partly Staffs.).
A. Bastardy maintenance orders 1852-67; births reg. 1866-1913; marriage notice books 1904-24; list of paupers 1892; parochial lists of outdoor poor (various parishes) 1873; reg. of paupers (alphabetical) c.1900-1907; out relief order books 1879-1913; relieving officer's outdoor relief appl. and report books 1889, 1910; rate book (various places, dates) 1895-1920; valuation lists (various places) 1875-97.
B. Min's 1836-1930; C'tee min's: Boarding-out 1900-29, Children's 1898; ledgers 1836-1912; parochial ledgers 1848-1912; treasurer's ac's 1927-30; list of Guardians and paid officers 1863; Guardians and RD councillors 1902-3; sup'an. reg. 1903-10; petty cash ac's 1928-30; financial statements 1892, 1921-30; stat's and weekly returns 1884-1913; out relief letter books 1873-1925, treasurer's books 1876-1911; relieving officer's outdoor relief weekly receipts and exp. 1904-16; Assessment C'tee min's 1862-81, 1886-1921, letter books 1873-1904; RSA min's 1872-93, parochial ledger 1873-79, 1885-87, financial statements 1876-91, letter books 1872-94; SAC min's 1892-1904, reports 1881-1901.
Public Record Office, Kew:
Corres. etc. 1835-1900 (missing 1856- Aug. 1871) [MH 12/10002-15]; staff reg. 1837-1921 [MH 9/12].

Oswestry [22] (local act 1790).
A. Baptisms reg. 1813-1923, burials reg. 1813-56; punishment book 1855-1910; Morda House adm. and discharge reg's 1916-25; births reg. 1857-1950; deaths reg. 1857-1955; reg. of lunatics 1923-33; lunatics: cert's for detention 1895-1933, reg. of mechanical restraint 1892-1935.
B. Act of Incorporation 1790; min's 1791-1930; Boarding-out C'tee min's 1910-40; ledgers 1890-1930; parochial ledger 1915-27; reg. of mortgages 1791-1833; Lunatics Visiting C'tee reports 1923-33; master's reports 1927-30; House C'tee visiting book 1919-75.
Oswestry Library.
B. 'Observations on bettering the condition of the poor in Oswestry', 1795 (MS); printed reports of the Society for bettering the condition of the poor in the Hundred of Oswestry ... 1812-23 (mainly stat's).
Public Record Office, Kew:
Corres. etc. 1834-1900 [MH 12/10019-34]; staff reg. 1837-1921 [MH 9/12].

Seisdon [14] (Bobbington, Rudge).
See under Staffordshire.

Shifnal [13] (partly in Staffs.).
A. Assessment C'tee: rate books (various places, dates) 1870-1926.
B. Min's 1836-1930; ledgers 1877-1930; parochial ledger 1916-27; treasurer's ac's 1925-30; boarding-out receipts and exp. 1923-30; service reg. 1860-1917; master's day book 1921-30; receipts and exp. 1926-35; garden and pig, wood etc. ac's 1902-37; clothing and materials ac's 1923-37; extra tea etc. ac's 1900-34; collector's ledger 1929-30; SAC min's 1913-21; RSA min's 1872-88.
Public Record Office, Kew:
Corres. etc. 1836-1900 [MH 12/10040-50]; staff reg. 1837-1921 [MH 9/15].

Shrewsbury [23] (Union incorporated 1784; amalgamated with **Atcham** in the 1870s and later known as **Atcham and Shrewsbury**; for records of all periods the **Atcham** entry should also be consulted).
A. Weekly return of paupers 1826-28; reg. of non-resident and 'foreign' poor 1824-25; reg. of appr's 1802-18, 1824-26; reg's of nurse children, various parishes 1784-1823; removals 1798-1830; settlement cert's 1705-62; settlement and bastardy exam's 1817-26; adm's 1784-1826; contributors' ledgers and ac's, payment for bastard children etc. 1784-1824 (naming contributors); adm's and discharges 1824-27, 1854-75; weekly muster rolls of in-poor (paupers named, by parish) 1834-42; indoor relief lists 1858-67, 1870-73; w'h. medical relief (Shrewsbury PLU) 1870-1; Kingsland w'h. adm's and discharges 1873-73; births reg. 1850-74; deaths reg. 1850-75; creed reg. 1870-75; marriage notice books 1837-71; Receiving Home adm. and discharge reg. 1916-48; Pen y Bont Home creed reg. 1912-43; Besford House creed reg. 1926-50.
B. General order books (min's) 1784-1878; order books (min's) for administration of w'h. 1809-26; letter books 1799-1814, 1823-39, 1865-71; min's (outdoor relief) and disciplinary actions in w'h. or against parish officers 1788-1824; ledgers 1823-71; parochial ledgers 1862-78; cash ac's (abstracts) 1786-1805; annual statements (abstracts of cash books) 1822-27; various returns and stat's 1784-99; weekly returns of paupers, parish totals (only) 1829-35; muster books (weekly returns, numbers only) 1823-28; master's reports 1853-72, day books 1864-75; receipts and exp. 1870-75; inventory 1866-74; clothing receipts and exp. ac's 1851-75; visitors' books 1791-96, 1859-63, 1868-74; out relief (paid by overseers), various parishes 1787-1822; medical relief reports 1838-1912; rating papers (St. Chad's) 1848-59; Children's Homes: superintendant's journal 1920-30.
Public Record Office, Kew:
Corres. etc. 1834-1871 [MH 12/10053-58]; staff reg. 1837-1871 [MH 9/15].

Shropshire continued

Stourbridge [5] (Cakemore, Halesowen, Hasbury, Hawne, Hill, Illey, Lapal, Ridgacre).
See under Worcestershire.

Tenbury [18] (Boraston, Burford, Greete, Nash, Whitton).
See under Worcestershire.

Wellington [8].
B. Min's 1836-1928; C'tee min's: Finance 1920-30, Boarding-out 1930-32, Children's Home 1913-30, Relief 1928; C'tee reports: House 1914-30, Contract 1922-3; ledgers 1863-71, 1875-83, 1905-30; treasurer's ledgers 1914-24; parochial ledger 1900-27; treasurer's book 1927-30; Guardians' attendance 1924-30, c'tee attendance 1928-30.
Public Record Office, *Kew:*
Corres. etc. 1834-1900 [MH 12/10059-81]; staff reg. 1837-1921 [MH 9/18].

Wem [2].
A. Relief order books 1871-77, 1886-95, 1908-12.
B. Min's 1836-1918; ledgers 1837-1930; parochial ledgers 1849-1916; master's receipts and exp. 1928-35, farm and pig ac's 1904-35, necessaries ac's 1921-35.
Public Record Office, *Kew:*
Corres. etc. 1835-1900 [MH 12/10085-100]; staff reg. 1837-1921 [MH 9/18].

Whitchurch (Incorporation 1792-1854).
A. List of parish appr's 1735-99; index of settlement exam's 1740-90; index of settlement cert's 1700-85.
B. Min's 1792-1800, 1817-25, 1832-44, 1846-54 (there is probably an overlap between the House of Industry and Board of Guadians min's).

Whitchurch [21] (PLU from 1854) (partly Ches., Flints.).
A. Rate books (36 vols.) 1910-28.
B. Min's 1858-64, 1868-1911, 1914-30; ledgers 1854-58, 1889-1922 (missing 1891); parochial ledgers 1891-99, 1908-27; staff service reg. 1875-1913; Assessment C'tee min's 1885-1927.
Public Record Office, *Kew:*
Corres. etc. 1835-1900 [MH 12/10101-15]; staff reg. 1837-1921 [MH 9/18].

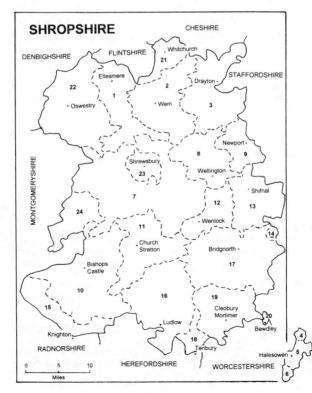

SOMERSET

See F. Chuk, 'Assisted immigrants', *Greenwood Tree* **10**.1, 1984/5.

Unless shown otherwise, records are at *Somerset Record Office, Taunton*.

There is a pioneering handlist, published 1949, but a few records have been added since. It includes a useful description of the main classes of records, with a scheme of classification which has since been adopted by many other record offices.

Ashton, Long see Bedminster.

Axbridge [4].

A. Reg. of children under control of Guardians 1910-19; adm. and discharge book 1873-1930 (gaps); reg. of adm's without orders 1914-32; births and deaths reg's 1838-68; baptisms reg. 1838-1903; medical exam. of inmates 1907-12, 1923-29, and of lunatics 1914-36; w'h. medical relief book 1910-11; creed reg. 1906-30; reg. of appl's and complaints by inmates 1914-36; offences and punishment book 1864-1903; casual adm. and discharge book 1910-11, 1928-30; ex-servicemen passing through 1926-7; out relief lists 1929-30; vac. reg. (Banwell 1881-86, Weston super Mare 1891-93); valuation lists, various places between 1899 and 1923.

B. Min's 1859-1929; C'tee min's: House 1907-20, 1923-30, Boarding-out 1926-30, Cheddar Cottage Home 1925-30, Electrical 1923-29, Assessment 1916-27, Farm 1920-23; ledger 1871-1930 (gaps); treasurer's ac's 1909-11, 1928-30; parochial ledger 1870-73, 1891-96, 1907-11; financial statement 1882; w'h. regulation 1914; Report books: porter's book 1873, 1911-2, master's 1911-2, 1922-28, fire brigade 1922-28, Visiting C'tee for lunatics 1913-33; w'h. ac's, (farm, provisions, inventories etc.) mostly 1910-30; list of officers 1926-30.

Public Record Office, Kew:
Corres. etc. 1834-1900 (missing 1887-1900) [MH 12/10118-47]; staff reg. 1837-1921 [MH 9/1].

Bath [7].

Bath City Record Office:

A. Removals C'tee cases 1904-15; cottage homes indoor relief lists (1896-1907) and creed reg's (1896-1901); relief order books, 1886-1928 (gaps); relief to unemployed 1922-27; maintenance exp. ledgers (1877-1905) and case books, most indexed (1891-1927); reg. of under-16's hired from w'h. 1851-97; bastardy order reg's 1844-1885; visits to appr's from w'h. 1882-1901; reg. of persons ordered to the w'h. 1878-86; pauper removal books 1845-63; reg. of children boarded-out 1869-95, 1909-18; nurse children and foster parents lists 1918-27; health records of children admitted to cottage homes 1911-18; reg. of persons receiving infants 1895-1930; vac. reg's 1910-1930; St. Martin's Hospital adm. and discharge books for casual paupers 1915-34 (unfit for production); burials reg. 1855-93; adm. and discharge for casual paupers, 1914/5, 1920/1 (unfit

for production); baptisms reg. 1899-1932; reg. of persons removed to other institutions 1903-18.

B. Min's 1836-1930; ledgers 1836-1909 (gaps); parochial ledgers 1848-1910; C'tee min's: General Purposes 1893-1902; Boarding-out 1869-1907; Assessment 1862-1923; Finance 1891-1904, SAC 1877-90; hospital and classification c'tee mins 1895-1901; joint and selection c'tee mins 1900-08; cottage homes superintendents' report books 1896-1915, inventory book 1896; loan book 1874-1900; stat. returns 1877-1914; letter books 1864-1903; Guardians: attendance book 1915-30, declarations 1894-1901, 1922-29; infant protection visitors' report books 1910-23; bye laws 1838, 1841-48; cash book 1892-1903; cottage homes clothing receipt and exp's book 1896-97; children's homes receipt and conversion ac's 1911-21; stores issue book, 1913-22; lunatic ledger 1903-05; collector's ac's book 1885-91; vac. officers' reports 1871-1914.

Public Record Office, Kew:
Corres. etc. 1834-1900 [MH 12/10158-96]; staff reg. 1837-1921 [MH 9/2].

Beaminster (Misterton, Seaborough).
See under Dorset.

Bedminster [5] (from 1899 as Long Ashton).

A. Annual returns of lunatics 1891-2; appr. indentures 1856-67; settlement and removal papers 1883-90; adm. and discharge book 1904-15; births and deaths reg's 1866-1930; reg. of appr's and servants 1851-67; indoor relief lists 1891-1918 (gaps) with index 1878-94; medical exam. of children 1914-5; w'h. medical relief book 1876, 1889-91, 1909-11; creed reg. 1901-30; reg. of clothing 1900-02; offences and punishment book 1871-1904 (see 'Bedminster Union Workhouse', Patricia Lindegaard, *Bristol and Avon FHS jnl.*, Autumn 1992, for list of boys punished 14 Feb. 1897); MO's report and exam. book 1875-1930 (gaps); casuals' adm. and discharge book 1910-12; appl. and report books (various) between 1890 and 1931; collector's ledger, receipt and exp. books 1926-30; vac. reg's 1861-98; various rate books 1861-1927 and valuation lists 1866-1925; war relief c'tee min's and appl's for assistance 1915-20.

B. Min's 1837-1930; C'tee min's: Finance 1921-29; Assessment 1891-1911, SAC 1877-1901, Building 1872-1903; ledgers 1836-1930 (gaps); parochial ledger 1854-1861; poor rate returns 1869-97, 1899-1916; repayment of teachers' salaries in w'h. school 1889-99; lunacy maintenance ac's 1881-1904; half yearly returns 1855-96; w'h. alterations 1846, 1875; supply tenders 1897; master's report book 1891-93, 1909-11, 1928-30; General Visiting C'tee report book 1879-1914 (gaps); various ac's (provisions etc.) and wages, C20; PLC letters 1840-43; quarry ac's 1837-8; Guardians' declarations 1900-29; lists of Guardians and officers 1872-1900, 1914-5; officers' bonds 1845-93; service reg. 1896-1930.

Public Record Office, Kew:
Corres. etc. 1834-1900 [MH 12/10204-38]; staff reg. 1837-1921 [MH 9/2].

Somerset *continued*

Bradford [20] (Freshford).
See under Wiltshire.

Bridgwater [3].
A. List of lunatics not in asylum 1919-30; adm. and discharge book 1916-31; births and deaths reg's 1866-1914; reg. of inmates 1916-31; creed reg. 1900-27; MO's report and exam. book 1926-31; casuals' adm. and discharge book 1930-1; appl. and report book 1929-30; out relief lists, various, 1912-30; collector's receipt and exp. book and ledger, various, 1910-30; vac. reg's, various, 1899-1930; reg. of persons receiving infants 1897-1929; reg. of infants received 1906-30.
B. Min's 1836-1930; C'tee min's: Finance 1927-30, House 1901-14, 1919-29, Boarding-out 1910-29, Special 1915-30, General Misc. 1868-97; ledgers 1837-1930 (gaps); treasurer's ac's 1891-1930 (gaps); mortgages 1923; reports on children boarded-out 1929; financial and stat. statements 1869-1910; report books: chaplain's 1928-32, master's 1910-1, 1927-29, General Visiting C'tee 1926-29; master's receipt and exp. book 1905-30; salaries and wages book 1914-30; w'h. provisions etc. ac's 1928-31; inventory book 1905-09, 1927; receipt and exp. books, various, 1910-30; collector's ledger, various, 1897-1930; infant life protection Inspector's report book 1909-30; list of officers and Guardians 1902-13; service reg. 1896-1930.
Public Record Office, Kew:
. Corres. etc. 1834-1900 [MH 12/10243-80]; staff reg. 1837-1921 [MH 9/3].

Chard [17] (partly Devon, Dorset).
A. Reg. of non-resident poor 1915-27; reg. of visits to appr's etc. 1901-18; reg. of children boarded-out 1906-12, 1914-20; adm. and discharge book 1891-1929 (gaps); births and deaths reg's 1848-1914; indoor relief lists 1893-4, 1911; medical exam. of children 1914-23; reg. of lunatics in w'h. 1880-1906; reg. of inmates 1899-1906; creed reg. 1913-30; ·offences and punishment book 1862-98; casuals' adm. and discharge book 1910-13; appl. and report book, various between 1891 and 1930; out relief list, various, 1881-1912; vac. reg's, various districts between 1871 and 1932; reg. of school exemption cert's 1905-22; Crewkerne census of children at school 1881; war relief c'tee min's and appl's for assistance 1915-6.
B. Min's 1836-1930; C'tee Min's: Finance 1890-1930, House 1892-1930, Boarding-out 1911-30, Rural District Education 1903-33, Infirmary and Cottage Homes 1914-5; ledgers 1836-1930 (gaps); parochial ledgers 1851-1928 (gaps); reg. of mortgages 1903-30; ac's of maintenance of children boarded-out 1911-26; LGB corres. 1876-86; financial and stat. statements 1868-85; report books: chaplain's 1877-1905, MO's 1902-12, SAC officer's report book (Ilminster) 1904-14, General Visiting C'tee 1897-1933, vac. officer's 1901-10, Inspector of Nuisances 1888-1902; master's report book 1911-2,

1927-32, day book 1912-15, receipt and exp. book 1910-22; salaries and wages receipt book 1924-30; provisions etc. ac's, C20; collector's ledger (Crewkerne) 1917-30; petty cash book 1892-94; LGB letters 1887-89; reg. of securities 1895-1912; MO's reports on school children 1909; SAC corres. 1910-19; list of officers 1858-91; service reg. 1891-96.
Public Record Office, Kew:
Corres. etc. 1834-1900 [MH 12/10285-317]; staff reg. 1837-1921 [MH 9/4].

Clifton.
See under Gloucestershire.

Clutton [8].
A. Claims for maintencance of pauper lunatics 1887-1902; reg. of lunatics in asylums 1890, and not in asylums 1913-18; annual returns of pauper lunatics 1896-1900, 1902-30; relief order book 1928-30; reg. of visits to appr's etc. 1880-98; adm. and discharge book 1841-1916 (gaps) (casuals 1929-30); reg. of attendance at w'h. school 1894-1900; births reg. 1839-1933; baptisms reg. 1874-1929; deaths reg. 1838-1927; reg. of appr's and servants 1851-80; medical exam. of children 1914-19, 1924-30; w'h. medical relief book 1890-92, 1907-13; cert's for detention of lunatics 1878-1902; creed reg. 1875-1930; cert's for employment of pauper nurses 1898-1900; offences and punishment book 1851-1904; appl. and report books (various) between 1891 and 1930; out relief lists, various between 1874 and 1930; collector's receipt and exp. books, various, 1923-30; vac. reg's, various, between 1871 and 1934; reg. of persons receiving infants 1909-16.
B. Min's 1836-1930; C'tee Min's: Finance 1874-1930; Relief 1895-98; ledgers 1837-1930 (gaps); treasurer's ac's 1911-13; claims for repayment of officers' salaries 1881-87; weekly returns 1881-87, 1909-12; weekly returns of persons chargeable 1878-93; reg. of relief on loan 1909-10; settlement etc. journey book 1868-78; corres. 1836-46; LGB corres. 1891-1929; MoH report on out relief 1928; report books: chaplain's 1857-74, 1900-24, MO's 1868-1914, General Visiting C'tee 1863-1909 (gaps), Lady Visitors' 1895-1917; master's report book 1842-1928 (gaps), receipt and exp. book 1929-30; salaries and wages book 1897-1930; w'h. ac's, dietaries, provisions, extras between 1879 and 1932; inventory book 1881-95; collector's ledger, various, 1922-30; Harptree plans 1901-21; return of sanitation salaries 1881-88; Farmborough rent ac's 1892-1900; SAC officer's reports, part, 1879-1913; Guardians' declarations 1894-1928; standing orders 1836-72.
Public Record Office, Kew:
Corres. etc. 1834-1900 (missing 1841-2, 1854-63, 1889-92) [MH 12/10320-40]; staff reg. 1837-1921 [MH 9/5].

Dulverton [1].
A. Reg. of children placed in service 1874-1914; removal orders 1853-79; recovery of relief 1912-30; list of outdoor paupers 1904-22; adm. and discharge

Somerset: Dulverton *continued*

book 1855-1930 (gaps) (casuals 1912-13, 1930);
births reg. 1866-1927; deaths reg. 1866-1930;
indoor relief list 1899-1930 (gaps); reg. of lunatics in
w'h. 1890-1915; MO's reports for detention 1884-
1915; creed reg. 1869-1930; reg. of inmates'
clothing 1864-91; reg. of wayfarers relieved 1880-
91; out relief lists and appl. and report book 1836-
1930 (gaps); abstract of out relief list 1913-18;
collector's receipt and exp. book 1907-30; school
fees appl's etc. 1877-84, 1891.

B. Min's 1836-1930; Boarding-out C'tee min's
1913-30; ledger 1836-1930 (gaps); treasurer's ac's
1928-30; parochial ledger 1865-1930 (gaps);
financial statements 1901, 1906-30; corres. 1836-
97; report books: MO's 1901-30, master's 1913-30
(gaps), matron's 1914, General Visiting C'tee 1903-
28; inventory book 1888-1932; dietary 1880-91;
clothing materials ac's 1911-31; relieving officer's
diary 1869-72; collector's ledger 1907-30; census
plans 1921; Assessment C'tee corres. 1863-4; reg.
of common lodging houses 1883-94; SAC officer's
reports 1883-1906; educational returns (incl. w'h.
school) 1879-86.

Public Record Office, Kew:
Corres. etc. 1835-96 [MH 12/10346-57]; staff reg.
1837-96 [MH 9/6].

Frome [11].
A. Relief order book 1889-94, 1907-12; reg. of
relief on loan 1862-70; reg. of children under control
of Guardians 1900; records of children apprenticed
etc. 1910-18; ag'mts by relatives to contribute 1911-
22; orders for contribution by relatives c.1842-1928;
maintenance orders (bastardy) 1844-72; list of
paupers 1889-1915; adm. and discharge book 1847-
1930 (gaps) (w'h. school 1849-60, Warminster
Union 1928-30, porter's 1916-33, casuals 1911-30);
births and deaths reg's 1836-1912; indoor relief list
1849-75, 1878-1919; medical exam. of inmates
1914-30; w'h. medical relief book 1850-1; notice to
coroner on deaths of lunatics 1900-09; reg. of
inmates 1913-22; creed reg. 1910-19; labour book
1857-63; reg. of inmates' own property 1911-32;
Whitewell Home: adm. and discharge book 1913-16,
indoor relief list 1913-19; out relief, various districts
1836-7; appl. and report books and out relief lists,
various districts between 1836 and 1919; relief on
loan record (Kilmersdon) 1864-66; reception orders
for lunatics: Frome 1920-29, Kilmersdon 1892-1903;
DMO relief lists, c.1888-1916; collector's receipt and
exp. book, Kilmersdon 1909-14; rate books: Frome
1880-1, 1887, Hardington 1860-78; valuation lists,
various, 1860's - 1880's; reg. of persons receiving
infants 1893-98, 1902-11; reg. of infants received
1898.

B. Min's 1836-1930; C'tee min's: House 1914-28,
Union 1836-44, 1894-1930; ledgers 1836-1930
(gaps); treasurer's ac's 1929-30; financial
statements 1882-1912; weekly returns 1837-1930
(gaps); pauper classification book 1905-07; reg. of
mortgages 1890-1; reports on boarded- out children

1914-26; reports on irremovable poor 1856-65;
porter's book 1876-80; report books: chaplain's
1880-1932 (gaps), MO's 1901-25, master's 1837-
1930 (gaps), nurse's 1926-30, C'tee of Lady Visitors
1894; Visiting C'tee for Lunatics 1890-1928 (gaps);
master's day book 1885-90, receipt and exp. book
1868-1915; salaries and wages 1900-30; officers'
dietary ac's 1902-22; w'h. provisions, extras etc.
(incl. coffins) ac's between 1872 and 1930;
Whitewell Home: superintendent's report 1913-20;
visitors' report book 1913-4, day book 1913-16,
provisions etc. ac's 1910-18; receipt and exp. book,
various districts, 1836, 1910-30; relieving officer's
diary 1910 and weekly report book (Rode) 1836;
pauper desciption book c.1836; Frome out-relief list
for vagrants 1869-73; collector's ledger (Kilmersdon)
1910-18; statement of contibutions in arrear (part)
1900-30; census plans 1901-11; report books: vac.
officer's 1912-18, Inspector of Nuisances' (Rode)
1864-73, SAC officer's (Nunney) 1900-06, infant life
inspector's 1891-1921; special expenses rate book
1887; Sanitation General C'tee min's 1893-99;
corres., various, between 1836 and 1930; reg's for
conduct of w'h. c.1879, 1914; list of Guardians and
officers 1839-1900; service reg's 1896-1929;
salaries etc. 1928-30.

Public Record Office, Kew:
Corres. etc. 1853-1900 (missing 1856-58) [MH 12/
10358-74]; staff reg. 1837-1921 [MH 9/6].

Keynsham [6] (partly Glos.).
A. Adm. and discharge book 1836-1930 (gaps)
(casuals 1882-84); births reg. 1836-90; baptisms
reg. 1890-1915; indoor relief lists 1848-9, 1929-33;
reg. of lunatics in w'h. 1902-30; creed reg. 1869-
1933; offences and punishment book 1838-95; vac.
reg. (part) 1917-36; rate book (Saltford) 1897-8;
various valuation lists 1863, 1866, 1882-1916;
school fees order book 1883-88; reg. of cowkeepers
1887-8; inspector's reports on infants 1898-1930.

B. Min's 1837-1930; C'tee min's: Finance 1904-30,
House 1836-1930, SAC 1877-90, Assessment 1862-
94; General 1897-1929; ledgers 1836-1930 (gaps);
parochial ledgers 1848-1901 (gaps); petty cash ac's
1913-30; financial statements 1887-1925, of exp.
1836-42, 1866-1914, and of ac's 1885-95; poor rate
returns 1891-1924; repayment of teachers' salaries
1889-1914; maintenance of indoor paupers elsewhere, C20; weekly returns 1927-30; yearly etc.
returns 1850-1930; returns on education of pauper
children 1904-09; w'h. alterations 1876-1926; reg. of
mortgages 1884-1905; out letters 1836-64; PLC
corres. etc. 1836-95; in letters 1870-73; treasurer's
ac's book 1928-30; report books: chaplain's 1872-
81, master's 1849-1928 (gaps), General Visiting
C'tee 1876-87, 1904-48, C'tee of Lady Visitors 1918-
30; master's day book 1848-61; salaries etc. 1917-
30; minor w'h. ac's C19-20; various returns of birth
and death 1888-93; list of buildings registered for
marriage 1837-1936; registration corres. 1836-95;
vac. officer's report book (1913-21) and returns
(1844-79); returns of assessable values 1899-1923;

Somerset: **Keynsham** *continued*

Sanitation: MO's report 1896, receipt and exp. returns 1883-94, in letters 1890-96, infectious diseases record 1891-96; reg'ns for w'h. 1914; lists of Guardians and officers 1836-1911; officers' bonds c.1918-1929; service reg. 1896-1930; reg. of officers' appointments 1888-1914; salaries 1927-30; sup'an. returns 1900-14.
Gloucester Library.
B. Ac's 1889-96; order for out relief 1895.
Public Record Office, Kew:
Corres. etc. 1834-1900 [MH 12/10377-400]; staff reg. 1837-1921 [MH 9/9].

Keynsham Out-relief Union.
A. Claims for maintenance of lunatics 1899-1915; annual return of lunatics 1891-1916; various cases papers (n.d.); out relief order book 1924-29; relief to aliens 1914-19; reg. of children boarded out 1910-19; appl. and report books 1927-30; out relief lists 1928-30; vac. reg. (part) 1917-36; war relief c'tee min's and appl's for assistance 1915-20.
B. Min's 1895-1930; C'tee min's: Finance 1904-30, Boarding-out 1910-30; ledgers 1895-30 (gaps); treasurer's ac's 1929-30; petty cash ac's 1895-97; financial statements 1895-1925; poor rate returns 1896-1925; weekly etc. returns 1895-1929; general boarding-out file 1910-17; in letters 1913-16; treasurer's ac's book 1924-29; relieving officer's receipt and exp. book 1927-30; list of Guardians and officers 1895-1921; officers' bonds 1907-30; annual sup'an. return 1911.

Langport [14].
A. Adm. and discharge books: general 1890-1919, mental defectives chargeable to Somerset C.C. 1916-31, casuals 1909-23; births reg. 1886-93, 1914-31; deaths reg. 1914-31; indoor relief lists 1913-16, 1919-21; medical exam. of children 1914-24; reg. of inmates 1910-30; creed reg. 1906-16; offences and punishment book 1871-99, 1923-31; appl. and report books (various) 1911-25; out relief lists 1899-1927 (gaps); medical relief list 1916; vac. reg. (Kingsbury 1911-36, W'h. district 1922-25).
B. Min's 1881-1930; C'tee min's: House 1922-30, Boarding-out 1910-30; ledgers 1855-1930 (gaps); parochial ledger 1904-15, 1917-27; financial state-ments 1921-30; rate collector's monthly statements 1919-27; LGB order re. child emigration 1911; porter's book 1913-20; report books: chaplain's 1885-1918, 1928-31, master's 1914-30, General Visiting C'tee 1885-1924, C'tee of Lady Visitors 1905-30; master's day book 1867-77, 1912-21 (with summary 1910-19); receipt and exp. book 1905-16, 1925-30; w'h. various ac's between 1868 and 1931; relieving officer's receipt and exp. books (part) 1865-1918; collector's ledger 1904-09, 1915-22.
Public Record Office, Kew:
Corres. etc. 1834-1900 [MH 12/10406-24]; staff reg. 1837-1921 [MH 9/10].

Mere [16] (Maiden Bradley, Kilmington, Stourton). See under Wiltshire.

Molton, South (pt. Exmoor). See under Devon.

Shepton Mallet [10].
A. Case papers (various); list of paupers 1898-1902; property tax assessments (part) 1864-67; adm. and discharge book 1853-1930 (gaps) (casuals 1915-22, 1927-30); births reg. 1866-90, 1914-26; deaths reg. 1866-90, 1914-30; births and deaths reg. 1891-1913; indoor relief list 1859-85; medical exam. of children 1911-16; cert's for detention of lunatics 1881-89; reg. of mechanical restraint 1895-1929; creed reg. 1888-1930 (gaps); reg. of inmates' property 1914-17; offences and punishment book 1887-1924; out relief books c.1836; appl. and report books (various) 1838-1929; out relief lists (various) 1836-1930; medical relief lists (various) 1891-1921; collector's receipt and exp. books (part) 1906-30; rate books (Shepton Mallet) 1886-1912; valuation lists (various) 1863-1912; SAC reg. of exemption cert's 1890-1908; vac. reg's (various) 1911-33.
B. Min's 1836-1930; C'tee min's: Finance 1908-13, House 1914-30, Boarding-out 1918-30, Cottage Homes 1929-30, SAC 1895-1903; ledgers 1836-1930 (gaps); parochial ledger 1909-27; financial statements 1903-08; precepts 1918-20; alterations to w'h. 1850; supplies contract prices 1902-16; file re. boarded-out children 1902-10; treasurer's ac's book 1927-30; porter's book 1857-72, 1877-82; report books: chaplain's 1905-31, MO's 1914-30, master's 1890-1, 1909-30, General Visiting C'tee 1904-27, C'tee of Lady Visitors 1900-22; master's receipt and exp. book 1924-30; salaries and wages book 1904-12; w'h. detailed ac's, and inventory book, between 1880 and 1930; relieving officer's receipt and exp. book (part) 1913-30; collector's ledger 1914-19, 1927-30; sanitation plans 1892; list of Guardians and officers 1907-29; service reg. 1896-1926.
Public Record Office, Kew:
Corres. etc. 1834-1900 [MH 12/10427-49]; staff reg. 1837-1921 [MH 9/15].

Sherborne [19] (Goathill, Marston Magna, Poyntington, Rimpton, Sandford Orcas, Trent). See under Dorset.

Taunton [13] (partly Devon to 1896).
A. Out relief order book 1893-97, 1907-28; list of paupers etc. 1875-79; adm. and discharge book 1871-1930 (gaps) (part indexed) (casuals 1910-30 (gaps)); births reg. 1836-1932; deaths reg. 1836-1947; indoor relief lists 1866-1930; medical exam's: inmates 1915-28, alleged lunatics 1914-29; reg. of mechanical restraint 1906-25; notices to coroner, deaths of lunatics 1901-29; creed reg. 1898-1926; inmates' record cards 1912-30; cert's of employment of inmates in sick wards 1914-27; reg. of appl's and complaints by inmates 1913-36; notices to friends re. illness or death 1914-18/9; vac. reg's (various) 1908-30; appl. and report books 1870's - 1928

(gaps); out relief lists (various) c.1870-1920's; DMO medical relief lists (part) 1886-91, 1905-27.

B. Min's 1836-1930; Finance C'tee min's 1914-30; ledger 1836-1930 (gaps); parochial ledger 1910-29; non-settled poor ledger 1886-1914; financial statements 1927-30; returns of persons chargeable 1913-29; rent sheet 1909; reg. of mortgages 1901-24; reports of removable poor 1908-25; rate collector's montly statements 1920-1; w'h. regulations 1896-1914; porter's book 1913-17, 1927-31; report books: chaplain's 1907-21, MO's 1898-1927, master's 1911-20, 1928-30, nurse's 1913-18, 1928-30, General Visiting C'tee 1901-26; master's day book 1913-17, 1929-33 (summaries 1892-98, 1903-34); w'h. detailed ac's between 1893 and 1930; inventory book 1893-1902; dietary for casual poor c.1925; sanitation byelaws (n.d.); list of Guardians and officers 1920-1; service reg. 1896-1930.

Public Record Office, Kew:
Corres. etc. 1834-1900 [MH 12/10452-82]; staff reg. 1837-1921 [MH 9/17].

Thornbury.
See under Gloucestershire.

Wellington [12] (partly Devon).
A. Reg. of children boarded-out 1902-14; reg. of appr's etc. 1907-12; settlement exam's 1842-46; births reg. 1867-1943; deaths reg. 1867-1914; indoor relief list 1846-53, 1869-70; medical exam. of inmates 1926-34, and of children 1928-32; creed reg. 1914-33; offences and punishment book 1851-1914; casuals' adm. and discharge book 1911-2; out relief lists (various) 1839-1916; valuation list (Wellington) 1869-70, 1881; vac. reg. (part) 1912-30; case files and min's: military exemption tribunals 1915-18.

B. Min's 1836-1930; C'tee min's: Children's 1902-30, House 1914-30, SAC 1877-1903; ledgers 1836-1930 (gaps); parochial ledger 1906-15; w'h. building ac's 1838-58; treasurer's ac's book 1928-30; Visiting C'tee for Lunatics report book 1920-34; salaries and wages receipt book 1913-27; garden and pig ac's 1918-41; record of w'h. exp. (Wellington and Milverton) 1836-39; Mantle Street Home: matron's report book 1913-34, day book 1918-30, provisions ac's 1919-30; letters re. valuation 1862-81; LGB sanitation letters 1887-92; list of Guardians and officers 1851-87; service reg. 1897-1930.

Public Record Office, Kew:
Corres. etc. 1834-1900 [MH 12/10487-512]; staff reg. 1837-1921 [MH 9/18].

Wells [9].
A. Relief order book 1874-89; adm. and discharge book 1912-14, 1923-25; indoor relief list 1891-93; medical exam. of children 1914-33; bathing reg's 1926-30; out relief list (part) 1928-30; collector's receipt and exp. book (part) 1918-30; war relief c'tee min's and appl's for assistance 1915-17.

B. Min's 1835-1930; C'tee min's: Cottage Homes 1902-29, Building 1836-7, Assessment 1876-87;

ledgers 1836-1930 (gaps); treasurer's ac's 1928-30; parochial ledger 1847-1927 (gaps); stat. returns 1847-49, 1904; appointment of overseers 1916-7; PLC etc. corres. 1836-45, 1901-03; corres. 1836-45; parochial rateable values 1895-97; MO's report book 1914-32; master's day book summary 1925-30; salaries and wages receipt book 1901-06; w'h. ac's between 1891 and 1932; reports of officer in charge of children's home 1904-28; relieving officer's receipt and exp. book 1928-30; collector's ledger 1916-30; sanitation: general ledger 1873-94, parochial ledger 1873-91; officers' bonds 1914.

Public Record Office, Kew:
Corres. etc. 1834-1900 [MH 12/10515-37]; staff reg. 1837-1921 [MH 9/18].

Williton [2].
A. War Relief c'tee min's and appl's for assistance 1915-6.

B. Min's 1839-1930; ledger 1872-1930 (gaps); treasurer's ac's 1927-30; parochial ledger 1870-1930; papers re. purchase of land for w'h. 1836-40; corres. 1836-45; service reg. 1896-1926.

Public Record Office, Kew:
Corres. etc. 1834-1900 [MH 12/10542-62]; staff reg. 1837-1921 [MH 9/19].

Wincanton [15] (partly Dorset to 1896).
A. Reg. of young persons placed in service 1899-1911; reg. of visits to appr's etc. 1899-1914; adm. and discharge book 1836-1912 (gaps) (casuals 1910-12); deaths reg. 1866-1907; indoor relief list 1891-93; reg. of inmates 1928-30; creed reg. 1869-1930 (gaps); leave of absence book 1914-19; out relief book (part) 1836; out relief lists (various) 1836-1930; vac. reg's, various between 1877 and 1932.

B. Min's 1836-1930; C'tee min's: House 1914-30, Boarding-out 1911-25; ledgers 1835-1930 (gaps); treasurer's ac's 1904-12; parochial ledgers 1849-1916 (gaps); financial statements 1900-25; ac's etc. 1849; report books: chaplain's 1902-24, master's 1911-13, General Visiting C'tee 1893-1914; salaries and wages receipt book 1912-30; w'h. detailed ac's between 1904 and 1930; Wincanton Girls' Home: visitors' report book 1929-30, inventory book 1918-29; parochial assessment files 1862-92; loan for sanitation c.1877; service reg. 1896-1930.

Public Record Office, Kew:
Corres. etc. 1850-1900 [MH 12/10567-83]; staff reg. 1837-1921 [MH 9/19].

Yeovil [18].
A. Claims for maintenance of pauper lunatics 1888-98, 1906-15; annual returns of lunatics 1871-1900; relief order book 1848-74; reg. of children under control of Guardians 1887; appr. indentures 1852-97; reports etc. re. boarded-out children 1913-29; orders for contribution by relatives 1896-1900; bastardy maintenance orders 1847-51; list of paupers 1860-1, 1901-14; adm. and discharge book 1836-1930 (casuals 1902-30); births and deaths reg's 1836-1914; indoor relief lists 1837-1930; medical exam. of children 1914-33; w'h. medical

relief book 1903-14; reg. of lunatics in w'h. 1874-90; reg. of mechanical restraint 1895-1932; notices to coroner, deaths of lunatics, 1913-31; creed reg. 1869-1930; bathing reg. 1914-27; offences and punishment book 1873-1941; reg. of addresses of paupers' friends 1906-23; settlement and removal orders 1875-1902; foster mothers' reports 1923-28; appl. and report book (various) 1837-1930; out relief lists (various) 1836-1930; MO's relief list 1837-1902; collector's receipt and exp. book (part) 1913-24, 1929-30; vac. reg's (various) 1876-1935; rate books (various) 1868-1927; valuation lists (various) 1862-1929; school fees appl. and report (part) and order book 1886-91; school fees receipt and exp. book 1885-93; War Relief C'tee min's and appl's for assistance 1915-16.

B. Min's 1836-1930; C'tee min's: Finance 1908-12, 1916-30, House 1895-1930, Allotments 1877-92, SAC 1877-1903, Vac. 1872-81, Boarding-out 1910-30, Assessment 1862-73, Cottage Homes 1914-30; ledgers 1836-1930 (gaps); parochial ledger 1849-1912 (gaps); non-settled poor ledger 1903-15; stat. and financial statements or returns, various, incl. parochial, 1836-1930; poor rate returns 1857-1930; precepts 1903-12, 1927; repayment of salaries 1859-72; papers re. management of children's home 1914-16; supplies contracts 1908-30; ac's re.

boarded-out children 1912-30; consents to receive paupers 1910-14; notices of appointment of overseers 1896-1924; overseers' balance sheets 1897-1916; rate collector's monthly statements 1904-22; ac's etc. 1836-1915; general in-letters 1837-42; in-letters from PLC etc. 1837-1922; out letters 1836-47; infectious diseases in w'h. 1879-98; w'h. management enquiry 1868; invitations to tender 1913-4; cert's of proficiency, w'h. teachers 1860-70; treasurer's ac's book 1906-30; porter's book 1838-1920; report books: chaplain's 1902-18, MO's 1864-1939, master's 1901-27, nurse's 1920-27, General Visiting C'tee 1837-40, 1908-22, Visiting C'tee for Lunatics 1877-1933; master's day book 1901-32; receipt and exp. book 1888-1923; detailed w'h. ac's between 1879-1930; inventory book 1869-1924; relieving officer's receipt and exp. book (various) 1845-1930; collector's ledger (part) 1910-30; returns of rental and rateable values 1863-99; sanitation: ledger (incl. parochial) 1873-96, receipt and exp. returns 1874-94; reg. of common lodging houses 1889; return of salaries 1859-89; water supply corres. 1887, 1891; Board regulations c.1894, 1903; officers' bonds 1884; service reg. 1896-1924.

Public Record Office, *Kew:*
Corres. etc. 1834-1900 (missing 1843-46, Mar. 1890 - Apr. 1891) [MH 12/10586-608]; staff reg. 1837-1921 [MH 9/19].

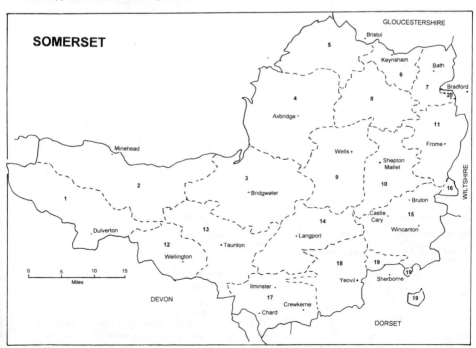

SOMERSET

GLOUCESTERSHIRE

Bristol
5
Keynsham
6
Bath
7
Bradford
20
4
8
Axbridge ·
11
Minehead
Wells ·
Frome ·
· Shepton Mallet
2
3
9
10
16
· Bridgwater
1
· Bruton
· Castle Cary
15
14
Dulverton
13
Wincanton
12
· Langport
Wellington
· Taunton
18
19
0 5 10 15
Miles
19
Ilminster ·
Yeovil ·
Sherborne
DEVON
17
Crewkerne
19
· Chard
DORSET
WILTSHIRE

WILTSHIRE

See M. Kay, 'Where's George?', *Greenwood Tree* **12**.1 (Winter 1986/7); J.S.W. Gibson, 'Assisted emigration of paupers from Wiltshire 1834-47', *Wiltshire FHS* **7** (Autumn 1982).

The PLU in which each parish lay is shown in the Wiltshire volume of the *National Index of Parish Registers*, **8**, 2 (Society of Genealogists, 1992); and also in Barbara J. Carter, *Location of Documents for Wiltshire Parishes* (7 parts, 1981-2).

Unless shown otherwise, records are at *Wiltshire Record Office, Trowbridge.*

Alderbury [24] (1836-95; from 1869 incl. **Salisbury;** in 1895 renamed **Salisbury**).
A. Rate surveys and valuations, various, between 1838 and 1926; collector's receipt and exp. books 1920-29; relief order books 1927-32; appl. and report books (part) 1924-31; adm., discharge and deaths reg's late C19-1925 (indexed); births reg. 1914-40.
B. Min's 1835-1923, 1927-30 (incl. Salisbury 1864-69); C'tee min's: Assessment 1862-1908, Building 1876-79, Technical Education 1891-95, Finance, House and Engineering 1899-1908, Boarding-out 1902-30, Children's 1909-26; ledgers 1835-1925; financial statements 1896-1920; w'h. provisions and consumption book 1915-6, 1929-32; necessaries and misc. book 1927-30; weekly returns 1906-09; PLC orders 1835-6; w'h. plans, ag'mts etc. 1836-1904; dietary 1841.
Public Record Office, Kew:
Corres. etc. 1834-1896 [MH 12/13639-56] (Alderbury), 1834-1869 [MH 12/13844-48] (Salisbury); staff reg. 1837-1921 [MH 9/1] (Alderbury), [MH 9/15] (Salisbury).

Amesbury [19].
A. Valuation lists, all parishes, 1885.
B. Min's 1835-39, 1845-1930; financial and stat. statements 1901-09; corres. 1877-1912.
Public Record Office, Kew:
Corres. etc. 1834-1896 [MH 12/13658-67]; staff reg. 1837-1921 [MH 9/1].

Andover [16] (Chute (Forest), Ludgershall, North Tidworth).
See under Hampshire.

Bassett, Wootton see **Cricklade**.

Bradford (on Avon) [12] (partly Som. to 1882).
B. Min's 1914-30; SAC min's 1900-03; year book 1901-2; PLC orders 1835, 1837; w'h. plans 1898; rules, n.d.; photographs 1930.
Public Record Office, Kew:
Corres. etc. 1834-1896 [MH 12/13668-84]; staff reg. 1837-1921 [MH 9/3].

Calne [9].
A. Lists of lunatics 1892-95; removal orders etc. 1892-3.

B. Min's 1834-1930; SAC min's 1877-1903; ac's and stat. 1881-92; weekly returns 1922-24; corres. 1888-1907; report of Visiting Commissioner in Lunacy 1891; outdoor relief schedule 1893; w'h. insurance, tenders etc. 1901, 1923.
Public Record Office, Kew:
Corres. etc. 1834-1896 [MH 12/13686-98]; staff reg. 1837-1921 [MH 9/4].

Chippenham [8].
See J. Philpot, 'Records of the [Chippenham] Union Workhouse,' *Wiltshire FHS* (Summer 1984).
A. Adm., discharge and deaths reg's 1881-1932 (indexed); births reg. 1866-1914.
B. Min's 1835-38, 1845-1930; C'tee min's: W'h. 1906-19, Finance 1906-30, Boarding-out 1912-34; w'h. provisions ac's 1835-48; financial statements 1844-1924 (gaps); corres. 1890-1925 (gaps); deeds etc. 1857-1966.
Public Record Office, Kew:
Corres. etc. 1834-1896 [MH 12/13699-717]; staff reg. 1837-1921 [MH 9/5].

Cirencester [4] (Kemble, Poole and Somerford Keynes, Marston Meysey, Poulton, Shorncott).
See under Gloucestershire.

Cricklade and Wootton Bassett [5].
A. Indoor relief ledger 1913-16.
B. Min's 1839-1930 (gaps); W'h. C'tee min's 1914-26; deeds etc. 1836-1914; chaplain's report book, from 1928.
Public Record Office, Kew:
Corres. etc. 1834-1896 [MH 12/13719-33]; staff reg. 1837-1921 [MH 9/5].

Devizes (1796-1828).
B. Various papers 1796-1828.

Devizes [14] (post-1834).
A. Adm. and discharge reg. 1899-1932 (indexed); births reg. 1848-1933; baptisms reg. 1871-1932; deaths reg. 1866-1939 (some indexed).
B. Min's 1835-1930 (gaps); Boarding-out C'tee min's 1910-27.
Public Record Office, Kew:
Corres. etc. 1834-1896 [MH 12/13735-49]; staff reg. 1837-1921 [MH 9/6].

Dursley [1] (Kingswood).
See under Gloucestershire.

Faringdon (Coleshill).
See under Berkshire.

Fordingbridge [25] (Damerham, Martin, Toyd Farm with Allenford, Whitsbury).
See under Hampshire.

Highworth and Swindon [6] (renamed **Swindon and Highworth** from 1899).
A. Valuation list (Rodbourne Cheney) 1906-28; adm. and discharge reg. 1899-1911, 1914-23 (indexed); births reg. 1866-1914; deaths reg. 1899-1911, 1914-23 (indexed), 1925.

B. Min's 1835-38, 1842-1930; C'tee min's: W'h. 1897-1927, 1929-33, General Purposes 1908-14, Farm 1914-32, Buildings and Repairs 1923-30; plan of institution 1930; financial statements 1904-5, 1912-16.
Public Record Office, Kew:
Corres. etc. 1834-1896 [MH 12/13751-71]; staff reg. 1837-1921 [MH 9/8, 16].

Hungerford [11] (Aldbourne, Gt. and Lit. Bedwyn, Buttermere, Chilton Foliat, Froxfield, Grafton, Ham, Hippenscombe, Hungerford, Ramsbury, Shalbourne, Tidcombe and Fosbury).
See under Berkshire.

Malmesbury [3] (partly Glos. to 1844).
A. DMO's relief book 1924-30; adm. and discharge reg. 1869-74; deaths reg's 1866-1933.
B. Min's 1835-69, 1874-1930; C'tee min's: Boarding-out 1915-30, W'h. 1917-30; financial statements 1915-28; MoH returns 1924-27; PLC orders 1842-48; tenders and contracts 1914; w'h. plans etc. 1914.
Public Record Office, Kew:
Corres. etc. 1834-1896 [MH 12/13776-88]; staff reg. 1837-1921 [MH 9/11].

Marlborough [10].
A. Annual returns of lunatics 1885-1893; removal papers 1845-74; relief order book 1910-17.
B. Min's 1845-1917 (gaps); W'h. C'tee min's 1914-30; ledger 1835-6; financial and stat. statements 1891-1904, 1906-14; stat. returns 1861-64, 1885-93, 1895-1901; weekly returns 1915-24; staff returns 1904-06, 1914-21; corres. 1909-22 (LGB 1899-1902); report on cost of maintaining paupers 1926; deeds 1837-98.
Public Record Office, Kew:
Corres. etc. 1834-1896 [MH 12/13789-99]; staff reg. 1837-1921 [MH 9/11].

Melksham [13] (from 1898 Trowbridge and Melksham).
See P. Blake, 'In and out of the workhouse', *Wiltshire FHS.* **44** (1992).
A. Adm. and discharge reg. 1911-44 (indexed); reg. of adm. of mental defectives 1916-48; reg. of removals and discharges 1917-50; births reg. 1878-1931; deaths reg. 1878-1949; inmates' property reg. 1914-54; offences and punishment book 1915-43.
B. Min's 1835-1930; C'tee min's: W'h. 1905-24, Finance 1928-30, Garden 1905-29; weekly returns 1929-30; corres., circulars etc. 1874-1912; w'h. plans etc. 1847, 1868; deeds etc. from 1873; photograph 1930; provisions consumption record 1855; Visitors' report books 1915-60; bed measurements 1848.
Public Record Office, Kew:
Corres. etc. 1834-1896 [MH 12/13800-17]; staff reg. 1837-1921 [MH 9/11].

Mere [20] (partly Som. and Dorset to 1896).
A. Appl's for relief 1912-29 (restricted access, not to be used for genealogical purposes).
B. Min's 1835-1930; SAC min's 1877-1903; financial and stat. records 1862-1930 (gaps).
Public Record Office, Kew:
Corres. etc. 1834-1896 [MH 12/13819-29]; staff reg. 1837-1921 [MH 9/13].

New Forest [28] (Bramshaw).
See under Hampshire.

Pewsey [15].
A. Valuation lists, various, 1898-1902; outdoor relief list (part) 1896, 1909-10.
B. Min's 1913-30; SAC min's 1895-1900; W'h. Visiting C'tee min's 1895-1914; financial statements 1899-1907; sample vouchers 1908-10; ac's book re. boarded-out children 1902-13; corres. etc. 1921; provisions consumption book 1923-30; DMO weekly relief report book 1926-30; deeds etc. 1836-1939.
Public Record Office, Kew:
Corres. etc. 18354-1900 [MH 12/13830-43]; staff reg. 1837-1921 [MH 9/13].

Ramsbury see **Hungerford**.

Romsey [27] (Melchet Park, Plaitford, West Wellow).
See under Hampshire.

Salisbury [23] (Incorporation 1770-1869; PLU from 1869, see **Alderbury**; renamed **Salisbury** in 1895).
See under **Alderbury**.

Stockbridge [26] (West Dean).
See under Hampshire.

Swindon see **Highworth**.

Tetbury [2] (Ashley, Long Newton).
See under Gloucestershire.

Tisbury [21] (partly Dorset until 1880s).
A. Pauper case records 1896-1930 (restricted; not to be used for genealogical purposes).
B. Min's 1835-1930 (gaps); financial statements 1839, 1924-5.
Public Record Office, Kew:
Corres. etc. 1834-1900 [MH 12/13849-61]; staff reg. 1837-1921 [MH 9/17].

Trowbridge and Melksham see **Melksham.**

Warminster [18].
A. Valuation lists mostly C20; non-resident and non-settled poor relief book 1845-47; outdoor relief lists 1857-59; annual returns of pauper lunatics 1842-99.
B. Min's 1835-1923; C'tee min's: SAC 1877-1902, Boarding-out 1910-34, W'h. 1921-29, Misc. 1902-27; survey and map 1838; ledgers 1836-1923; financial and stat. papers 1836-99; year books 1902-3, 1910-1; letter books 1857-90; deeds etc. 1799-1840; PLC orders etc. 1837, 1868; papers re. burial service dispute 1846-7; SAC byelaws 1900; w'h. plans etc. 1913-19.

Public Record Office, *Kew:*
Corres. etc. 1834-1896 [MH 12/13863-80]; staff
reg. 1837-1921 [MH 9/18].

Westbury and Whorwellsdown [17].
See P. Blake, 'Deaths in Westbury and Whorwells-
down Poor Law Union Workhouse, 1836-40',
Wiltshire FHS **27** (Oct. 1987).
A. Copy of returns of deaths in w'h. held in Public
Record Office 1836-40.
B. Min's 1835-1925; W'h. C'tee min's 1914-21,
1928-30; financial and stat. statements 1892, 1897,
1899, 1907; letter book 1848-72; dietary 1890.
Public Record Office, Kew:
Corres. etc. 1834-1900 [MH 12/13881-90]; staff
reg. 1837-1921 [MH 9/18].

Wilton [22].
A. Outdoor relief book (part) 1836.
B. Min's 1835-1930 (gaps); PLC orders 1835-42.
Public Record Office, Kew:
Corres. etc. 1834-1896 [MH 12/13892-902]; staff
reg. 1837-1921 [MH 9/19].

Wokingham (Hurst, Shinfield, Swallowfield,
Wokingham).
See under Berkshire.

Wootton Bassett see **Cricklade.**

**Wiltshire Joint Poor Law Establishment
Committee.**
B. LGB order 1912; Min's, letter books and ledger
1912-25; deeds and plans 1913-4.

WILTSHIRE

WORCESTERSHIRE

Unless shown otherwise, records are at
Hereford and Worcester Record Office H.Q.,
Spetchley Road, Worcester

General papers relating to several or all unions:
A. Exam. and removal cert's C17-19.
B. Deeds 1891-1955; general orders 1836-47;
Union returns on rateable values 1873-89 and
assessments 1874; PLC papers (HM Treasury)
1834-46; Min's of various joint c'tees under 1894
LG Act; mortgages 1902-25; 'Palfrey collection'
scrapbook on Unions etc.; dietaries 1687-1974.

Alcester [12] (Abbots Morton, Feckenham,
Inkberrow, (Upper) Ipsley, Oldberrow).
See under Warwickshire.

Bromsgrove [6] (partly Warws., Shrops., Staffs.).
See N. Land, *Victorian workhouse: a study of the
Bromsgrove Union workhouse 1836-1901* (1990).
A. Rate books 1915-26.
B. Min's 1836-1930; parochial ledger 1901-14;
financial statements 1847-75; collectors' monthly
statements 1926-29; sup'an. reg c.1896-1930.
Public Record Office, Kew:
Corres. etc. 1834-1896 [MH 12/13903-27]; staff
reg. 1837-1921 [MH 9/3].

Bromwich, West (Oldbury, Warley).
See under Staffordshire.

Bromyard [9] (Acton Beauchamp, Edvin Loach,
Lower Sapey).
See under Herefordshire.

Cleobury Mortimer [7] (Bayton, Mamble, Rock).
See under Shropshire.

Droitwich [11].
A. Rate book (St. Andrew's) 1898-9; receipt and
exp. book (St. Peter's) etc. 1836-47.
B. Min's 1836-1922; ledger 1836-1921; parochial
ledger 1848-1927; service reg. c.1896-early C20;
overseers' receipts and exp. 1885-1905; health/diet
papers 1687-1974 (sic).
Public Record Office, Kew:
Corres. etc. 1837-1896 [MH 12/13930-56]; staff
reg. 1837-1921 [MH 9/6].

Dudley [1] (formerly Worcs.).
See under Staffordshire.

Evesham [17] (partly Glos.).
A. Reg. of children 1901-30; births reg. 1914-44;
deaths reg. 1866-1914; servants' reg. 1920's;
affiliation book etc. 1830-42; rate book 1856.
B. PLC etc. orders 1836-51, 1924; Guardians'
photo 1929; deeds 1891-1955; conveyance 1879;
SAC byelaws 1880-1900.
Public Record Office, Kew:
Corres. etc. 1834-1896 (missing 1848-51) [MH
12/13997-14013]; staff reg. 1837-1921 [MH 9/6].

Worcestershire continued

Kidderminster [5] (partly Staffs., Shrops.)
(** indicates also available on microfilm at
Kidderminster Library.
A. Appr. indentures, mostly C19; rate books
(Wolverley) 1924-5; deaths reg.** 1866-84, 1895-
1919; creed reg's late C19-1918; children's home
creed reg. 1915-36; adm. and discharge reg.** 1904-
31 and 1910-41 (sic); creed and inmates reg., mid
C19-20; relief order book (n.d.); discharge book
1895-1904; appl. and report book 1912-3; school
fees receipt and exp. book 1886-1902; relief order
book 1908-9; reg. of infants 1909-29; Upper Arley
assessment schedule 1839; valuation lists (Broome
1879-97, Chaddesley Corbett 1879-1913 (with rate
book, n.d.), Rushock 1887-97); marriage notice book
1837-56.
B. Min's 1836-1928; C'tee min's: Assessment
1862-1927, W'h. Extension 1881-86, Boarding-out
1910-29; parochial ledgers 1847-1909; financial
statements 1879-1910; House C'tee reports and
master's report and journal 1914-30; PLC order
1836; sup'an. reg. c.1896-1920; overseers' receipt
and exp. book 1921-27; deeds etc. 1891-1955; reg.
of contracts (n.d.); letter books 1836-61; PLB letters
1836-52; Guardians' attendance reg. 1878-94;
wages receipt book 1929-35; rate return 1904-5;
order check book (sic) 1908; pauper classification
book 1894-1910; relieving officer's voucher list
1900-06; weekly returns 1913-4, 1929-30;
Kidderminster Infirmary annual reports** 1870-1932.
Public Record Office, Kew:
Corres. etc. 1834-1896 [MH 12/14016-37]; staff
reg. 1837-1921 [MH 9/9].

Kings Norton [3] (partly Warws., Staffs.;
amalgamated with **Birmingham** 1910-11).
Birmingham Central Library (Archives):
A. Vac. reg's (King's Norton 1878-1921, Edgbaston
1880-1918, Harborne 1893-1900, Smethwick 1918-
1922); returns of infant deaths: King's Norton 1872-
1922, Edgbaston 1878-1922, Harborne 1878-1907,
Smethwick 1908-1923; casuals adm. and discharge
reg. 1901; removal orders from Birmingham and
other parishes 1823-27; out relief list 1851; Cottage
Homes reg's (closed for 100 years): children 1887-
1924, deaths 1901-46.
B. Min's 1836-1912; 'various' c'tee and sub-c'tee
min's; relieving officer's appl. book 1849.
Public Record Office, Kew:
Corres. etc. 1834-1896 [MH 12/14039-74]; staff
reg. 1837-1921 [MH 9/9].

Ledbury [14] (West Malvern, Mathon).
See under Herefordshire.

Martley [10].
B. Min's 1863-1917, 1926-30; deeds etc. 1777-
1876; valuation list (Leigh) (n.d.); reg. of officers and
service reg's late C19-20; ac's (Shelsey
Beauchamp)1848-70; RSA min's 1872-82; w'h.
drainage plan 1895; Union division 1899.

Public Record Office, Kew:
Corres. etc. 1834-1896 [MH 12/14079-100]; staff
reg. 1837-1921 [MH 9/11].

Newent [18] (Redmarley d'Abitot, Staunton).
See under Gloucestershire.

Pershore [16].
A. Creed reg. 1907-30; reg. of infants 1921-30.
B. Min's 1835-1925; C'tee min's: SAC 1877-87,
Assessment 1863-77, Boarding-out 1912-30, House
1896-1914; PLC orders etc. 1845; overseers' ac's
book 1832-1909; receipts and exp. 1836-45;
insurance policy 1882; bonds 1882, 1892; salaries'
reg. 1920's; stat. abstracts 1837-53; dietary sheets
etc. 1687 (sic)-1974; w'h. ac's 1846; orders to pay
from poor rate 1845-47; ledgers 1835-1928; letter
books 1885-1908; Guardians' attendance reg. 1899-
1930; reports of House c'tee 1914-29; parochial
ledger 1847-80.
Public Record Office, Kew:
Corres. etc. 1834-1896 (missing 1840-47) [MH
12/14103-14]; staff reg. 1837-1921 [MH 9/13].

Shipston on Stour [21] (Batsford, Blockley,
Shipston on Stour, Tidmington, Tredington).
See under Warwickshire.

Solihull [4] (Yardley).
See under Warwickshire,

Stourbridge [2] (partly Staffs., Shrops.).
Staffordshire Record Office, Stafford:
A. Out-relief order books 1870-1929; removal
orders, Cradley, 1843-44; w'h. adm. and discharge
books 1842-92 (vagrants 1870-89); deaths reg.
1868-87; appr. reg. 1846-88; indoor relief lists 1837-
92; creed reg's 1869-1900; relieving officer's appl.
and report books 1837-1929; relief lists, receipts and
exp. c.1837-1926; vac. reg's 1853-99; poor rate
books 1837-95; valuation lists 1847-97.
B. Min's 1836-1929; Finance C'tee min's 1899-
1926; other c'tee min's 1893-1927; ledgers 1892-
1929; parochial ledgers 1894-1929; financial
statements 1895-99; stat. returns 1902-27; pauper
classification books 1847-1907; collectors' monthly
statements 1876-1911; letter books 1836-98;
treasurer's receipts and exp. books, 1867-1930; w'h.
master's reports 1866-1915; master's ac's 1873-
1905; DMO relief books 1870-1929; collectors'
ledgers 1876-1929; contracts for w'h. 1843-1905;
appl's for posts of master and matron 1880;
statement of population, rateable value, paupers and
maintenance 1893; misc. printed returns and reg. of
Guardians 1836-82.
Dudley Archives and Local History Service,
Coseley.
Some records, as yet unsorted.
Hereford and Worcester Record Office,
Worcester:
B. W'h. plans 1902-05; Union boundaries C19;
letters, ac's etc, late C19; petition against proposed
division (n.d.); min's of Joint C'tee (MOH
compensation case) 1896.

Worcestershire: Stourbridge *continued*

Public Record Office, *Kew:*
Corres. etc. 1834-1896 [MH 12/14134-64]; staff reg. 1837-1921 [MH 9/16].

Stow on the Wold [23] (Daylesford, Evenlode).
See under Gloucestershire.

Stratford on Avon [22] (Alderminster).
See under Warwickshire.

Tenbury [8] (partly Shrops., Heref.).
A. Births reg. 1927-30; deaths reg's 1866-1914, 1927-30; reg. of inmates 1930.
B. Min's 1836-1930; conveyance 1837, 1839.
Public Record Office, *Kew:*
Corres. etc. 1834-1900 [MH 12/14168-78]; staff reg. 1837-1921 [MH 9/17].

Tewkesbury [19] (Bredon, Bredon's Norton, Chaceley, Conderton, Overbury, Pendock, Teddington).
See under Gloucestershire.

Upton upon Severn [15].
A. Births reg. 1836-66; punishment book 1875-1932; valuation (Birtsmorton) 1826-1908; out relief paid 1836-48; list of non-settled poor 1840.
B. Min's 1835-1903, 1906-26; C'tee min's: House 1926-30, Boarding-out 1920-30; master's report book 1924-28; chaplain's report book 1836-1933; PLC orders 1835; letters 1872; election poster 1850; stat. abstracts 1836-48; sup'an. reg. c.1896-1930; parish expenses 1857; various health papers 1837-57; deeds etc. 1891-1955.
Public Record Office, *Kew:*
Corres. etc. 1835-1896 [MH 12/14179-99]; staff reg. 1837-1921 [MH 9/17].

West Bromwich see **Bromwich, West**.

Winchcombe [20] (Cutsdean).
See under Gloucestershire.

Worcester [13].
A. Baptisms reg. 1929-71; reg. of children placed out 1926-34; creed reg. 1894-1958; punishment book 1902-58; deaths reg. 1895-early C20; medical relief book 1923-43; reg. of children 1913-45; relief lists 1911-61; case papers early C20 (index 1920); index to unemployment appl's 1921-23; collector's receipt and exp. book 1838-48.
B. Min's 1917-30; C'tee min's: Finance 1919-30, House 1926-48, Building 1926-30, Settlement and maintenance 1926-30, Boarding-out 1923-30, Cottage Homes 1926-37, Relief 1926-37 (with agenda book etc. 1926-30, and various others 1923-30; Service reg. 1895-40; ac's book (poor fund) 1910-17; map of Union farm (n.d.); petitions against consecration of burial ground (n.d.); cottage homes reg'ns 1894; chaplain's report book 1893-1948; summary of day books 1929-53; weekly returns 1928-51; requisition books 1929-48; visitors' book 1918-33 (and inspection books 1925-51); Ladies C'tee visiting book 1922-59; receipt and exp. ac's book 1923-45; receipt and exp. books 1929-46; necessaries ac's 1926-28; various clothing ac's 1920-59; garden ac's book 1913-60; MO's report books 1920-56.
Public Record Office, *Kew:*
Corres. etc. 1834-1896 [MH 12/14202-28]; staff reg. 1837-1921 [MH 9/19].

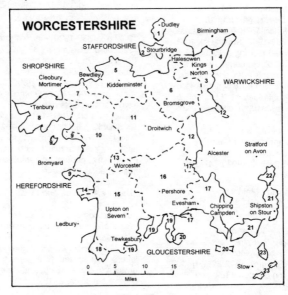

WALES

ANGLESEY

There was a major alteration in Union boundaries in 1852. Parts of south-west Anglesey were in the **Caernarvon** Union.

Anglesey [1] (see also **Holyhead**).
Anglesey Area Record Office (Gwynedd Archives and Museum Service), Llangefni.
A. Out relief records 1848-1919; children 1869, 1883, 1911-30; settlement papers 1833-58; adm. and discharge books 1887-1918; births reg's 1915-17; indoor relief lists 1904-15 (gaps); w'h. medical relief book 1907-18; relief to casual poor 1904-17; out relief records 1837-1929; vac. cert's 1879-90 (+ returns for various parishes).
B. Min's 1837-1930; ac's 1845-1929; lunacy records 1854-64; stat. 1852-1929; corres. 1845-1929; letter books 1892-1909; master's report and journal 1901-05, 1907-18, reports 1914-17; matron's report 1914; Visiting C'tee report book 1893-1912, 1914-18 and their reports on lunatics 1906-18; w'h. ac's 1900-18; assessment papers (various); SAC papers 1878-82; infant life protection papers 1909-29; sanitation papers (n.d.).
Public Record Office, Kew:
Corres. etc. 1852-96 [MH 12/15673-90]; staff reg. 1834-1921 [MH 9/1].

Bangor and Beaumaris [3] (partly Caernarvons.).
Anglesey Area Record Office (Gwynedd Archives and Museum Service), Llangefni.
A. MO 1888-98; appl. and report books (n.d.); outdoor relief lists abstract 1906-30; valuation lists (1839 Bangor only), 1890-1927; vac. papers 1879-1932; appr. indentures 1878-96; settlement papers 1890-1924; adm. and discharge book 1891-1932; indoor relief lists 1920-31; inmates' exam. book 1924-31; creed reg. 1892-95; births reg. 1846-1938; deaths reg. 1901-19; notices to coffin maker 1925-34; notices to clergyman re. illnesses 1899-1933; notices to MO 1914-32; reg. of mechanical restraint 1892-1934; punishment book 1898-1917; reg. of inmates' property 1916-34; addresses of paupers' friends 1916?; reg. of lunatics 1891-98; MO's exam. book (lunatics) 1914-26; relief order book (Beaumaris) 1928-31; relieving officer's receipt and exp. (part) 1926-31; district medical relief book (Gaerwen) 1923-30; collector's receipt and exp. book 1925-37; rateable values (Anglesey only) 1908-11.
B. Min's 1837-58, 1904-30; c'tee mins: Assessment 1862-1927, Finance 1887-1927, SAC 1877-1893, W'h. 1904-14, House 1914-28; RSA 1874-91; ledgers 1837-1900, 1925-29; parochial ledgers 1885-1918; letter books 1837-75, 1879-1930; abstract of out relief 1906-30; external orders, various; report books of w'h. masters 1915-38; chaplain's reports 1914-30; lady visitors' books 1898-1929; reg's, stores etc. (n.d.); w'h. MO's

reports 1888-1902; mortgages 1900-25; stat. 1881-1926; appointment of officers 1888-1929; PLB orders and letters etc. 1837-1904; relief to casual poor 1913-31; lunatics' visitors book 1887-1918.
Public Record Office, Kew:
Corres. etc. 1834-96 [MH 12/15964-92]; staff reg. 1834-1921 [MH 9/2].

Carnarvon [2] (Llanidan: Llanfair yn y Cwmmwd, Llangaffo, Llangeinwen, St. Peter's Newborough).
Anglesey Area Record Office (Gwynedd Archives and Museum Service), Llangefni; see also under Caernarvonshire.
A. Relief order book 1924-30; appl. and report book 1906-7; outdoor relief list 1925-6; collector's receipt and exp. book 1922-30; vac. reg. 1890-1906, 1913-22; list of rateable values (Anglesey) 1910.
B. Collector's ac's 1899-1931; list of rateable values (Anglesey parishes) 1910; relieving officer's receipt and exp. book 1922-30; receipt and exp. book 1928-30.

Holyhead [1] (formed out of Anglesey).
Anglesey Area Record Office (Gwynedd Archives and Museum Service), Llangefni.
A. Lunacy returns 1909-15; out relief 1867-1920; children 1908-30; adm. and discharge books 1870-1931 (abstracts 1916-32); school adm. and discharge book 1872-75; indoor relief list 1870-1916; MO's exam. papers 1914-32; w'h. medical relief books 1870-1912; creed reg. 1899-1906, 1930; relief to casual poor 1907-31.
B. Min's and ac's 1852-1930; stat. 1868-1929; treasurer's receipt and exp. book 1882-1930; ac's 1870-1930; reports 1870-1928; papers of officer in charge of children's home, n.d.; relieving officer's papers 1860-1931; papers of collector to the Guardians 1879-1933; vac. papers 1912-25; assessment papers 1862-1927; RSA papers 1872-91.
Public Record Office, Kew:
Corres. etc. 1852-96 [MH 12/15691-705]; staff reg. 1852-1921 [MH 9/8].

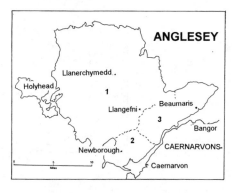
ANGLESEY

Llanerchymedd .
Holyhead
1
Llangefni .   Beaumaris
3
Bangor
2
Newborough .   CAERNARVONS-
Caernarvon

BRECKNOCK or BRECONSHIRE

Unless shown otherwise, records are at *Powys Record Office, Llandrindod Wells.*

Brecknock [4].
A. List of paupers 1926-29.
B. C'tee min's: Assessment 1862-80, Finance and General Purposes, Relief and Special 1898-1930, RSA 1872-94; reg. of mortgages 1926-28; parochial ledgers 1881-86; abstract of ac's 1926-29.
Public Record Office, Kew:
Corres. etc. 1834-96 [MH 12/15707-33]; staff reg. 1837-1921 [MH 9/3].

Builth [3] (partly in Radnors.).
A. Lists of officers and paupers 1923.
B. Min's 1902-07; C'tee min's: Visiting 1914-47, Assessment 1902-27, RSA 1872-94.
Public Record Office, Kew:
Corres. etc. 1834-96 [MH 12/15734-46]; staff reg. 1837-1921 [MH 9/3].

Crickhowell [8].
B. Min's 1836-43, 1872-96; reg. of mortgages 1911-28.
Public Record Office, Kew:
Corres. etc. 1834-96 [MH 12/15747-67]; staff reg. 1837-1921 [MH 9/5].

Hay [5] (partly in Herefs., Radnors.).
A. Adm. and discharge books 1909-32; births reg's 1914-48; deaths reg's 1914-64; reg's of inmates 1916-54; creed reg's 1903-26; inventories of inmates' property and cash 1922-29.
B. PLB/LGB orders 1866-78; chaplain's report book 1897-1968; SAC min's 1892-1903.
Public Record Office, Kew:
Corres. etc. 1834-96 [MH 12/15769-82]; staff reg. 1837-1921 [MH 9/8].

Llandovery [2] (Llandulas-in-Tyr Abbot, Llanwrtyd). See under Carmarthenshire.

Merthyr Tydfil [7] (Penderyn, Vaynor). See under Glamorgan.

Neath [6] (Ystradfelte, Ystradgynlais). See under Glamorgan.

Rhayader [1] (Llanwrthwl). See under Radnorshire.

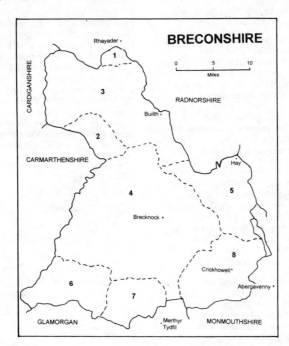

BRECONSHIRE

CAERNARVONSHIRE

Unless shown otherwise, records are at *Caernarfon Area Record Office (Gwynedd Archives and Museum Service), Caernarfon.*

Bangor and Beaumaris [1] (Aber, Bangor, Llandegai, Llanfairfechan, Llanllechlid).
See under Anglesey.

Caernarvon [3] (partly in Anglesey).
A. Creed reg's 1901-10, 1921-38; other w'h. records post-1914; outdoor relief abstracts 1887-1908; vac. reg's 1853-72; deaths of infants under 12 months 1885-98; births reg. (vac.) 1872-1902.
B. Min's 1907-29; ledgers 1911-31; parochial ledgers 1923-27.
Public Record Office, Kew:
Corres. etc. 1834-96 [MH 12/15998-16022]; staff reg. 1837-1921 [MH 9/4].

Conway [2] (partly in Denbighs.).
B. Min's 1879-1930; C'tee mins: Assessment 1907-27, SAC 1877-1903; ledgers 1901-30; parochial ledgers 1898-1910; financial statements 1915-27; treasurer's books 1908-30; letter books 1879-1913, 1923-25; LGB orders 1877-1893; deeds etc. 1885-1930; lists of Guardians and officers 1905-29; poor rate returns 1911-22.
Public Record Office, Kew:
Corres. etc. 1834-96 [MH 12/16023-46]; staff reg. 1837-1921 [MH 9/5].

Festiniog [6] (Beddgelert, Dolbenmaen, Llanfihangel-y-Pennant, Penmorfa, Trefblys, Ynyscynhaiarn).
See under Merioneth.

Llanrwst [4] (Eglwys Fach: Maenan; Ysputty Evan: Tir Evan, Eidda, Trebrys; Llanrwst: Bettwys y Coed, Dolwyddelan, Llanrhychwyn, Penmachno, Trefriew, Tre Gwydir).
See under Denbighshire.

Pwllheli [5].
A. Adm. and discharge books 1853-1923; reg. of young persons apprenticed from w'h. 1877-1911; pauper lunatics cert's and exam. books 1859-1908; other w'h. records (various); abstract of outdoor relief 1885-1920; births reg. (vac.) 1853-1914.
B. Min's 1837-44, 1847-1930; C'tee min's: Assessment 1878-1914, RSA 1872-93, various others, incl. Finance, Visiting etc. 1905-17; ledgers 1892-1920; letter books 1849-56, 1871-78.
Public Record Office, Kew:
Corres. etc. 1834-18 [MH 12/16052-72]; staff reg. 1837-1921 [MH 9/13].

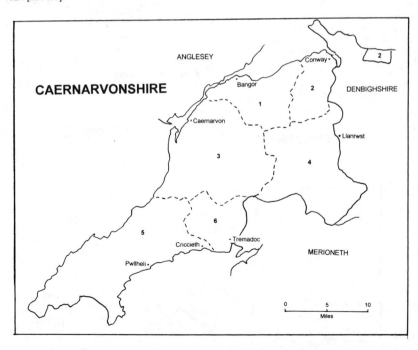

CARDIGANSHIRE

See E.A. Benjamin, 'Of paupers and workhouses', *Ceredigion* **10** (1990); A.E. Davies, 'The New Poor Law in a rural area', *Ceredigion* **8** (1978); and R. Davies, 'Poor Law Board correspondence (1834-1909)', *Dyfed F.H.J.* **4**.2 (1991) (from PRO MH 12 records, referring to Cards. and Pembs.).

Unless shown otherwise, records are at *Cardiganshire/Ceredigion Record Office (Dyfed Archive Service)*, Aberystwyth.

Aberaeron [3].
A. Vac. books 1899-1919; relief order books and lists 1912-34.
B. Min's 1837-1930; financial records 1837-1930.
Public Record Office, Kew:
Corres. etc. 1834-96 [MH 12/15783-95]; staff reg. 1837-1921 [MH 9/1].

Aberystwyth [2].
See D. Jones, 'Pauperism in the Aberystwyth Poor Law Union', *Ceredigion* **9** (1980).
A. Vac. reg's 1853-1918; relief lists 1916-34; appl. and report books 1926-35; births reg. 1883-1930; deaths reg. 1883-1914; valuations 1897-1900.
B. Min's 1869-1930; financial records 1881-1930; master's records 1912-36.
Public Record Office, Kew:
Corres. etc. 1836-96 [MH 12/15796-816]; staff reg. 1837-1921 [MH 9/1].

Cardigan [5] (partly in Pembrokes.).
A. Adm. and discharge books 1856-1935; MO's records 1901-35; births and deaths reg. 1901-35; indoor relief lists 1861-1935; outdoor relief lists 1868-90.
B. Min's 1837-84; financial records 1842-89; master's records (journals etc.) 1907-31; provisions ac's 1897-1935; visitors' books 1898-1935.

Pembrokeshire Record Office, *Haverfordwest.*
A. Lists of paupers 1901/2, 1906/7 (with abstract of ac's).
B. Min's 1927-30 (indexed); Assessment C'tee min's 1913-27 (indexed); inventory book of the institution 1917-35; ledgers 1923-27; lease of 1868; w'h. insurance policy 1840; corres. re. charity 1924-37; photo's of Guardians 1904, c.1910, 1929.
Public Record Office, Kew:
Corres. etc. 1834-1896 (missing 1887-8) [MH 12/15817-43]; staff reg. 1837-1921 [MH 9/4].

Lampeter [7] (partly in Carmarthens.).
A. Vac. reg. 1889-98; adm. and discharge books 1877-1941; MO's records 1881-1937; births and deaths reg. 1878-1938; appl. and report books 1876-1935; relief lists 1877-1938; rate books (some parishes only) 1890-1904.
B. Min's 1837-1930; financial records 1837-1930; master's records 1877-1938; day books 1900-38; provisions ac's 1918-49; visitors' books 1899-1935.
Public Record Office, Kew:
Corres. etc. 1834-96 [MH 12/15845-57]; staff reg. 1837-1921 [MH 9/10].

Machynlleth [1] (Scybor y coed).
See under Montgomeryshire.

Newcastle-in-Emlyn [6] (partly in Carmarthens., Pembrokes.).
A. Vac. reg's 1910-30; relief order books 1910-30.
B. Min's 1837-1930; financial records 1837-1930.
Public Record Office, Kew:
Corres. etc. 1834-96 [MH 12/15949-62]; staff reg. 1837-1921 [MH 9/12].

Tregaron [4].
B. Min's 1868-1930; financial records 1870-1931.
Public Record Office, Kew:
Corres. etc. 1837-96 [MH 12/15858-71]; staff reg. 1837-1921 [MH 9/17].

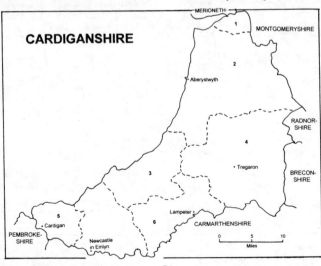

CARMARTHENSHIRE

Unless shown otherwise, records are at *Carmarthenshire Record Office (Dyfed Archive Service), Carmarthen.*

Carmarthen [4].
B. Min's 1927-30; ledgers 1917-30.
Public Record Office, Kew:
Corres. etc. 1834-96 [MH 12/15872-95]; staff reg. 1837-1921 [MH 9/4].

Lampeter [2] (Llanbydder, Llancrwys, Llanllwni, Pencarreg).
See under Cardiganshire.

Lland(e)ilofawr [5].
B. Min's 1836-1930; sub c'tee min's 1928-42; ledgers 1912-28.
Public Record Office, Kew:
Corres. etc. 1834-96 [MH 12/15922-36]; staff reg. 1837-1921 [MH 9/10].

Llandovery [6] (partly in Brecknock).
B. Min's 1840-1950 (sic); ledgers 1911-25.
Public Record Office, Kew:
Corres. etc. 1834-96 [MH 12/15937-48]; staff reg. 1837-1921 [MH 9/10].

Llanelli/Llanelly [7] (partly in Glamorgan).
B. Min's 1836-1930.
Public Record Office, Kew:
Corres. etc. 1834-96 [MH 12/15897-920]; staff reg. 1837-1921 [MH 9/10].

Narberth [3] (Castle-dyran, Cily Maenlwyd, Cyffie, Eglwys-Cimmin, Egremont, Henllan Amgoed, Llanboidy, Llandysilio, Llangan, Llanvalteg, Marros, Pendine).
See under Pembrokeshire.

Newcastle-in-Emlyn [1] (Cenarth, Cilrhedyn, Llanfihangel ar Arth, Llangeler, Pemboyr).
See under Cardiganshire.

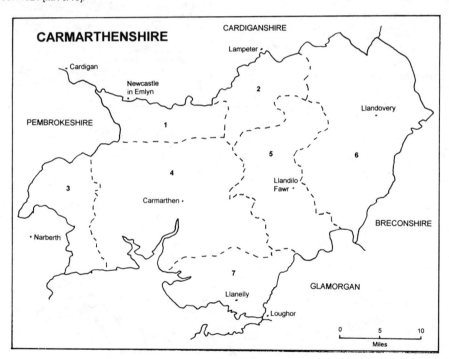

DENBIGHSHIRE

There is a map and parish table in *Hel Achau* **10** (Summer 1983); and see S. Blackwell 'Was your ancestor in the Union?', *Hel Achau* 22 (Summer 1987) for a list of inmates in the 1881 census.

Unless shown otherwise, records are at *Clwyd Record Office, Ruthin.*

Conway [1] (Llandrillo yn Rhos, Eirias).
See under Caernarvonshire.

Corwen [4] (Llanfihangel Glyn-y-Myfyr, Cerig-y-Druidion, Llangwm, Bryn Eglwys, Llandisilio, Glyn Traian, Llanarmon-Dyffryn-Ceiriog, Llansantffraid-Glyn-Ceirog).
See under Merioneth.

Llanfyllin [7] (Carreghova, Llanarmon mynidd Mawr, Llancadwallader, Llangedwyn, Llanrhaidr yr Mochant).
See under Montgomeryshire.

Llanrwst [2] (partly in Caerns.).
B. Min's 1837-1930; ledgers and ac's 1837-1929.
Public Record Office, Kew:
Corres. etc. 1835-96 [MH 12/16075-86]; staff reg. 1837-1921 [MH 9/10].

Oswestry (Chirk, Llansillin).
See under Shropshire.

Ruthin [5].
B. Min's 1837-44; printed yearbooks 1886-1902 (gaps); financial statements 1866/7; PLC order 1837.
Public Record Office, Kew:
Corres. etc. 1834-96 [MH 12/16987-103]; staff reg. 1837-1921 [MH 9/14].

St. Asaph [3] (Abergele, Betwys-yn-Rhos, Denbigh, Henllan, Llanddulas, Llanfair Talhaearn, Llanefydd, Llansannan, St. George).
See under Flintshire.

Wrexham [6] (partly in Flints., Cheshire).
A. Reg's of children under control of Guardians 1891-1930; reg's of inmates 1892-1930; adm. and discharge books 1890-1920; births and deaths reg's 1886-1914; maternity reg. 1912-30.
B. Annual printed booklets 1877-1928 (gaps); sup'an. reg's 1857-1934; ledgers and ac's 1837-1929; staff reg's 1915-30; MO's report books 1912-30; master's report books 1989-1919.
Wrexham Library.
A. Printed lists of out-door poor relieved 1907, 1910.
B. Printed ac's 1856.
Public Record Office, Kew:
Corres. etc. 1834-96 (missing 1851-56) [MH 12/16104-28]; staff reg. 1837-1921 [MH 9/19].

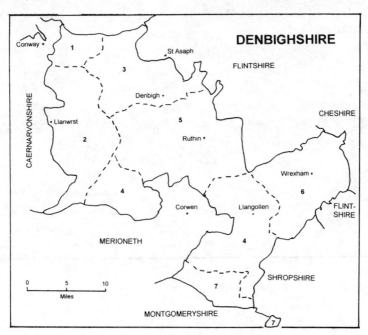

FLINTSHIRE

See S. Blackwell, 'Was your ancestor in the Union?' (1881 census), *Hel Achau* **22** (Summer 1987) and 'Clwyd parishes in each Poor Law Union', *Hel Achau* **10** (Summer 1983). The places constituting Hawarden, Holywell and St. Asaph PLUs are also listed in A.G. Veysey, *Guide to the Flintshire Record Office* (1974) (*GFRO*).

Unless shown otherwise, records are at *Clwyd Record Office, Hawarden*.

Entries are selected from *GFRO*, pp. 24-30; particularly for the 'B' category this will provide considerably more detail.

Boughton, Great [3] (Hawarden and Higher Kinnerton, to 1853).
See under Cheshire.

Ellesmere [5] (Hanmer, Overton).
See under Shropshire.

Hawarden [3] (formed 1853; partly Cheshire until 1871).
A. Creed reg. 1914-21; casuals' adm. and discharge books 1916-32; appl. and report books 1922-30; out-relief lists 1921-30 (abstract 1913-39); vac. reg's 1909-30; rate books; Buckley (Hawarden) 1898-1900, Hawarden 1862-1926, Higher Kinnerton 1876, Hope 1899-1925, Llanfynydd 1912-26, Marford and Hoseley 1926, Saltney 1863-91, East Saltney 1921-26, West Saltney 1912-26, Sealand 1896-1926, Shotton 1914-25, Treuddyn 1884-1926; valuation lists (various places) between 1863 and 1925.
B. Min's 1857-1930 (gaps); C'tee min's: Finance 1915-30, Ladies' 1914-30, SAC 1897-1904; ledgers 1919-30; returns of persons chargeable 1927-30; maintenance of boarded-out children ac's 1910-29; overseers' balance sheets (Hawarden) 1887-1903; treasurer's books 1924-30; master's day book 1927-32 (summary 1924-32); receipt and exp. 1919-32; wages receipt book 1918-31; farm ac's 1918-32; clothing ac's 1917-32; provisions ac's 1928-32; valuation lists between 1863 and 1925 (see *GFRO*); Hawarden RSA: min's 1872-94, ledgers 1873-95, parochial ledger 1875-91.
Public Record Office, Kew:
Corres. etc. 1853-96 [MH 12/16165-75]; staff reg. 1853-1921 [MH 9/8].

Holywell [2].
F. = Flint; H. = Holywell; M. = Mold; W. = Whitford (districts).
A. Relief order books 1908-30; appr. indentures of pauper children 1845-78; reg. of appr's 1845-52; reg. of children boarded-out 1896-1914; records of exam's and removal orders 1868-97; adm. and discharge books 1840-1934 (index 1840-47) (casuals 1879-80, 1895-1930); w'h. school reg's 1872-96; births reg's 1848-1917; deaths reg's 1848-1936; indoor relief lists 1847-1917; medical exam. books: inmates 1901-24, children 1925-33; medical

relief books 1898-9, 1909-10; reg's of lunatics 1890-96, 1928-48; notices to coroner of death of lunatics 1906-31; MO's cert's 1885-91; creed reg's 1893-1937; index to inmates' individual record papers 1914-21; indoor labour books 1840-52; clothing reg. 1869-86; punishment book 1915-44; record of ex-servicemen passing through casual wards 1917-8; out-relief books 1837; appl. and report books: H. 1837-1925, M. 1879-1928, W. 1837-74, 1912, 1922; out-relief lists: F. 1837-46, H. 1848-1921, M. 1837-1927, W. 1837-1929; abstracts: H. 1919-26, M. 1887-98, W. 1895-1929; out-relief for vagrants: M. 1867-71; DMO relief lists: F. 1842-60, H. 1848-70, 1913-4, M. 1837-68, W. 1848-57, 1878-88, Llanasa 1849-52; vac. reg's: F. 1883-94, H. 1911-19, M. 1853-1944, W. 1904-44; vac. officer's report books 1914-22 (summary 1900-19); rate books: Brynford, Northrop, Whitford, 1913-26, Caerwys, Holywell Rural (Bagillt), 1917-26, Cilcain 1915-24, Flint 1876, Gwaenysgor 1926, Halkyn, Holywell Rural (Greenfield), Newmarket, 1915-26, Holywell 1875-86, Holywell Urban 1913-18, Holywell Rural 1916-26, Llanasa 1891, 1921-26, Mold 1875, Mold Rural 1913-25, Nannerch 1888-90, 1926, Nercwys 1925, Ysceifiog 1880-2, 1916-26; valuation lists between 1868 and 1923 (see *GFRO*); infant life protection: reg. of infants received for reward 1909-21.
B. Min's 1837-41, 1846-1930; various c'tee min's 1842-1930 (see *GFRO*); lists of Guardians and officers 1876-87; officers' bonds 1837-98; in-letter books 1837-42; out-letter books 1843-1928; master's report books 1843-1935, day books 1912-32 (summaries 1868-1930), receipt and exp. books 1867-1932; wages receipt books 1922-31; farm, garden, pig, oakum, stone and wood ac's 1864-1945; inventory books 1847-1932; clothing ac's 1840-1936; provisions ac's 1842-1940, necessaries and misc. ac's 1867-1932; relieving officer's receipt and exp. books: F. 1837-51, H. 1913-25, M. 1904-27, W. 1881-83, 1906-13; collector's ledgers: H. 1900-33, M. 1900-12, W. 1921-35; receipt and exp. books: W. 1837-48, 1894-1904, H. 1892-1931, M. 1901-09, 1925-27, PLU 1842-45, 1877-1901; Assessment C'tee min's 1862-79; overseers' receipt and exp. books (11 parishes) 1867-1927; SAC min's 1885-91, 1897-1904; school fees appl. and report books 1888-92, order books 1882-91, receipt and exp. book 1883-91; Holywell RSA: H. Nuisance C'tee min's 1861-72, RSA 1881-85 (draft 1872-78, 1883-90); various report books 1872-94 (see *GFRO*).
Public Record Office, Kew:
Corres. etc. 1834-96 [MH 12/16176-205]; staff reg. 1837-1921 [MH 9/8].

St. Asaph [1] (partly Denbighshire).
A. Adm. and discharge books 1842-1933; births reg's 1866-1947; deaths reg's 1866-1913; indoor relief lists 1840-1916; creed reg's 1869-1928, (Cottage Home) 1914-30; appl. and report books: St. Asaph 1919-30, Rhyl 1927-8; out-relief lists: St. Asaph and Rhyl 1924-30; rate books: Tremeirchion

Flintshire: St. Asaph *continued*

1866, 1878, 1926, Rhuddlan 1910-26, St. Asaph 1914, 1926, Bodelwyddan, Bodfari, Cwm, Dyserth, Meliden, Waen, 1926; infant life protection: inspector's reports on infants 1910-29.

B. Min's 1841-1930 (missing 1916-7); C'tee min's: Finance 1927-30, House 1925-29, Boarding-out 1910-30; declarations by Guardians 1895-98; ledgers, ac's etc. 1837-1930; collectors' monthly statements: Bodfari 1926-7, Rhuddlan 1906-27; salaries reg. 1921-30; treasurer's books 1922-24, 1928-30; master's report books 1843, 1865-1921; visiting c'tee report book 1906-25; garden and pig ac's 1912-44; inventory books 1849-89; relieving officer's receipt and exp. books: St. Asaph 1920-30, Denbigh 1924-26; collector's ledgers: St. Asaph 1900-29, Rhyl 1912-27; receipt and payment books: St. Asaph 1919-28, Abergele 1917-30, Rhyl 1912-31; vac. officer's report book 1928-34; Assessment C'tee min's 1863-1907; valuation lists between 1877 and 1927 (see *GFRO*); St. Asaph Rural Sanitary Authority: ledgers 1872-94, parochial ledgers 1874-94, MO's annual reports 1875-94.

Public Record Office, Kew:
Corres. etc. 1834-96 (missing Mar. 1889 - Feb. 1891) [MH 12/16131-61]; staff reg. 1837-1921 [MH 9/1].

Whitchurch (to 1852).
See under Shropshire.

Wrexham [4] (Abenbury Fechan (Wrexham), Bangor, Erbistock, Hope Threapwood, Trydden (Mald), Worthenbury).
See under Denbighshire.

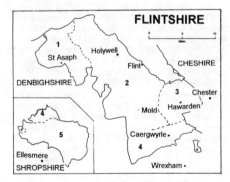

FLINTSHIRE

GLAMORGAN

At *Glamorgan Record Office, Cardiff,* PLU records are on restricted access, reg's closed for 100 years, other classes for 30. Collections are extensive and only min's and other main series records which are likely to include references to individuals are listed below. Records are at an outside repository, so at least a week's notification is required.

Bridgend and Cowbridge [5].
Glamorgan Record Office, Cardiff.
A. Adm. and discharge reg's 1921-2, 1925-27, 1929-30; creed reg's 1904-14, 1924-34; reg. of lunatics 1890-1912; list of paupers 1894-5, 1915; Bridgend Cottage Homes: Adm. and discharge reg's 1879-1923, 1927-30; creed reg's 1879-1919.
B. Min's 1836-1930 (missing 1847, 1856, 1917-8); Bridgend Cottage Homes 1878-1909, 1914-30.
Public Record Office, Kew:
Corres. etc. 1834-96 [MH 12/16209-40]; staff reg. 1837-1921 [MH 9/3].

Cardiff [6] (partly in Monmouths.).
Glamorgan Record Office, Cardiff.
A. List of paupers 1853-1912; children in institutions and schools (alphabetical) 1889-1915; rate books: Penarth 1880-1903, Cogan 1895-6, 1899-1902, Llandough 1882-84, 1896-1902.
B. Min's 1836-1930.
Public Record Office, Kew:
Corres. etc. 1834-96 [MH 12/16246-40]; staff reg. 1837-1921 [MH 9/4].
See also **Pontypridd** PLU.

Cowbridge see Bridgend.

Gower [2].
West Glamorgan County Archive Service, Swansea.
A. Births reg. 1914-30; creed reg's 1869-98, 1912-45; punishment book 1914-23; Brynau parish supplemental valuation 1895, 1909-18.
B. Min's 1896-1914, 1917-30; Assessment C'tee min's 1900-26; printed statements or abstracts of ac's 1898-1910; ledgers 1895-1930; treasurer's ledger 1922-27; parochial ledgers 1898-1922; misc. papers, ag'mts, ac's re. building of Penmaen w'h. 1860's; master's day book summary 1922-43; clothing ac's balance 1924-43; hiring and service, terms of contract 1899-1912; Gower RSA min's 1872-92; map of Swansea Bay 1867.
Public Record Office, Kew:
Corres. etc. 1857-96 [MH 12/16313-24]; staff reg. 1837-1921 [MH 9/7].

Llanelli [1] (Lougher).
See under Carmarthenshire.

Glamorgan continued

Merthyr Tydfil [4] (partly in Brecknock).
See Mrs Tydfil Thomas, *Poor Relief in Merthyr Tydfil Union in Victorian Times* (1992).
Glamorgan Record Office, Cardiff.
A. Adm. reg's 1878-1931; discharge reg's 1881-84, 1888-1934; adm. and discharge reg's 1857-76, 1878-81, 1883-86, 1889-1904, 1909-11, 1922-24; list of paupers 1850-1913 (gaps); creed reg's 1868-79, 1886-90, 1894-1932, Pontsarn sanitorium 1913-1914; reg. of inmates, Pantyscallog and Windsor Houses 1912-33; reg. of lunatics 1890-1930.
B. Min's 1836-1930 (missing 1877-8, 1885, 1892).
Public Record Office, Kew:
Corres. etc. 1834-96 [MH 12/16326-51]; staff reg. 1837-1921 [MH 9/11].
See also **Pontypridd** PLU.

Neath [3] (partly in Brecknock).
West Glamorgan County Archive Service, Swansea.
A. *Neath W'h.* Adm. and discharge reg's 1867-71, 1873-1931; births reg's 1871-1931; deaths reg's 1871-1932; reg's of lunatics 1890-1940; creed reg's 1913-31; indoor relief lists 1910-30; punishment book 1914-22. *Neath Union or Bryncoch Cottage Homes.* Adm. and discharge reg's 1878-1955; indoor relief lists and abstracts 1886-1955 (gaps); creed reg's 1877-1946; punishment book 1890-1918; outdoor relief lists 1917, 1919-30, order book 1927-34. *Vac. reg's.* Aberavon 1925-29; Abergwynfi 1919-28; Glyncorrwg 1902-29; Margam 1853-1928; Ystradfellte 1896-1901; notices of removal to vac. officer 1925-29.
B. Min's 1853-57, 1877-91 (gaps), 1893-1930; C'tee min's: Finance 1898-1930, SAC 1877-1903, Assessment 1923-26, Bryncoch Cottage Homes 1909-30, Penrhiwtyn Infirmary 1920-30, Boarding-out 1911-30, Out-relief 1928-31, Relief-on-loan 1927-30, Visitors' 1915-20, Contracts 1920-29,

Neath and Llantwit sanitary 1866; ledgers: 1917-30, collector's 1922-29, parochial 1917-26; statement of ac's 1913-4; master's reports 1917-30, day books 1915-32, receipt and exp. 1915-30, wages 1912-26, sup'an. 1926-30. *Bryncoch.* MO's report 1929-50; visitors' books 1925-54; staff appointments and salaries 1901-33; wages books 1914-31; clothing balance books 1924-55; farm stock and ac's 1925-49; photo of children c.1900. *Vac. records.* Summary of Vac. Officer's proceedings 1899-9131; Glyncorrwg: proceedings 1926-34, reports 1920-30, return of deaths of infants 1917-24, yearly return 1929-32; Margam: reports 1871-1930, return of deaths of infants 1872-1916, yearly return 1917, 1929-32. RSA. Min's 1876-81, 1886-93.
Public Record Office, Kew:
Corres. etc. 1834-96 [MH 12/16354-86]; staff reg. 1837-1921 [MH 9/12].

Newport [7] (Llanvedow, Rhydgwern).
See under Monmouthshire.

Pontardewe.
West Glamorgan County Archive Service, Swansea.
A. Adm. and discharge reg's 1915-19, 1925-43 (casuals 1925-27, 1930-1; casual paupers 1924-5); creed reg's 1902-21, 1927-48; births and deaths reg's 1914-43; reg's of persons of unsound mind 1923-42; reg's of inmates 1917-41; inventory of property of deceased inmates 1914-44; inmates' property reg. 1928-34.
B. Min's 1875-1930; Assessment C'tee min's 1875-1928; ledgers 1875-1930; parochial ledgers 1875-1926; treasurer's ac's 1913-21; clothing receipt and exp. books 1925-43; RSA min's 1883-93; bath reg'ns n.d. c.1920.
Public Record Office, Kew:
Corres. etc. 1875-96 [MH 12/16426-36]; staff reg. 1837-1921 [MH 9/13].

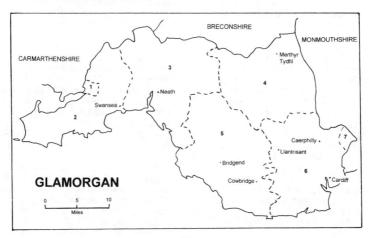

Glamorgan *continued*

Pontypridd (formed 1863, from outlying parishes of Cardiff and Merthyr PLUs).

Glamorgan Record Office, Cardiff.

A. Reg's of lunatics 1887-1930. Central Homes, Pontypridd: adm. and discharge reg's 1897-1931; creed reg's 1888-1931; births reg's 1865-1929; deaths reg's 1891-1926; reg's of inmates 1927-32. Pontypridd Cottage Homes: adm. and discharge reg's 1892-1930; creed reg's 1892-1936; Llwynypia Hospital: creed reg's 1903-31; births reg's 1914-33.

B. Min's 1863-74, 1882-1930.

Public Record Office, Kew:
Corres. etc. 1862-96 [MH 12/16393-418]; staff reg. 1863-1921 [MH 9/13].

Swansea [2].

West Glamorgan County Archive Service, Swansea.

A. Deaths reg. 1924; creed reg's 1868-70, 1903-27 (gaps); list of paupers and abstract of ac's 1872-85, 1891-95; school adm. and discharge book (boys) 1865-70; school attendance books (boys and girls) 1876-7; indoor relief book 1836-40; reg. of young persons 1865-70; punishment book 1855-80; reg. of lunatics 1890-99; valuation lists: unspecified 1890, Brynmelin 1910-26, Clase 1863-1928 (large gaps), Cockett 1890-95, 1910-28, Ffynone 1910-29, Landore 1910-28, Llandeilotalybont 1883-87, Llansamlet 1877-1928, Morriston 1910-28, Penderry 1878-1901 (gaps), Swansea: Castle 1911-28, East 1910-28, Higher and Higher and Lower 1880-95, 1901-?, St. Helen's 1910-28, St. John's 1880-1928, St. Thomas 1880-1901, Town 1890, 1903-10, Victoria 1910-28.

B. Min's 1849-51, 1860-1930 (gaps); C'tee min's: Finance 1881-85, 1888-1907, Assessment 1862-66, 1873-90, Visiting 1856-1910; PLB letter books 1859-69; remuneration of officers 1910-29; Duties and Salaries C'tee reports 1891, 1914-18; master's report and journal 1842-1914 (gaps), half yearly reports 1914-47, stat's 1914-48; chaplain's book 1854-58, 1874-88; porter's book 1837-47; weekly returns (poor relief) 1929-30; order book 1905-10; provision book 1839-47 (gaps); pauper classification book 1868-75; medical relief book 1876; Ladies' C'tee visiting book 1894-97; receipts and exp. 1897-1911; House C'tee: matron's reports 1914-48, superintendent nurse's reports 1914-38; MO's reports 1929-31; Cottage Homes visitors' books 1906-26 (gaps); House Visiting C'tee reports 1915, 1923-4; Graig House: weekly reports 1915-19, food requisitions 1915-17; ledgers: 1838-40, 1842-44, general 1847-52, 1858-1927, parochial 1852-1906, non-settled poor 1853-87, 1895-1911; treasurer's ac's 1902-27 (gaps); Rhyndwyclydach overseers of the poor receipt and exp. book 1837-63. *RSA.* Min's 1876-94; surveyors' reports 1884-96; treasurer's ac's 1892-94; cash book 1887-90; ledgers 1874-92.

Public Record Office, Kew:
Corres. etc. 1834-96 [MH 12/16437-74]; staff reg. 1837-1921 [MH 9/16].

MERINETH

Unless shown otherwise, records are at *Dolgellau Area Record Office (Gwynedd Archives and Museum Service), Dolgellau.*

Bala [2].

A. Deaths reg. 1914-46.

B. Min's 1837-1930; ac's and finance: ledgers 1837-1917, returns and orders etc. 1879-82, 1897, 1899, 1902, 1908-12, 1915, 1917, 1919, corres. 1837-71, misc. 1876, 1880-1; w'h.: bills and receipts 1879-80.

Public Record Office, Kew:
Corres. etc. 1836-96 [MH 12/16478-85]; staff reg. 1837-1921 [MH 9/2].

Corwen [3] (partly Denbighs.).

A. Adm. and discharge reg. 1913-4; indoor relief list 1913-23; reg. of children and foster parents 1901.

B. Min's 1837-1930; ac's and finance: ledgers 1837-1930, parochial ledgers 1848-1927, outdoor relief list (abstracts) 1870-1914, financial statements 1872-1903, service reg. 1897-1901, Assessment C'tee 1911-27; w'h.: weekly return of relief 1879-81, master's report book 1897-99, 1902-04, 1908-10; returns of births and vac's 1923-28; letter books etc. 1839-49, 1861-71, 1875-1931.

Public Record Office, Kew:
Corres. etc. 1834-96 [MH 12/16486-501]; staff reg. 1837-1921 [MH 9/5].

Dolgellau/Dolgelley [4] (partly Montgomerys.).

B. Min's 1837-1905 (gaps), 1917-29; ac's and finance: ledgers 1910-12. 1928-30, Finance C'tee min's 1927-30, misc. 1852-3, 1902; Assessment C'tee min's 1862-80; SAC book 1878-1903.

Public Record Office, Kew:
Corres. etc. 1834-1896 (missing Aug. 1871-76) [MH 12/16503-19]; staff reg. 1837-1921 [MH 9/6].

Ffestiniog [1] (partly Caernarvons.).

A. Appl. and report books 1908-27, 1929-30; relief order books 1911-37; outdoor relief list 1913; adm. and discharge books 1847-54, 1867-85, 1894-99, 1901-08, 1911-28; indoor relief list 1860-63; punishment book 1898-1918; pauper's loan book 1881-1919; pauper's friends address book 1915-48; MO's exam. book 1916-29; births reg. 1914-34; medical exam. of children and infants 1919-22; reg. of lunatics 1888-1930; reg. of mechanical restraint 1896-1925; valuation lists 1910, 1917-8.

B. Min's 1842-69, 1876-1931; Boarding-out C'tee min's 1912; House, Assessment and Finance C'tee min's 1914-27; official communications 1831-46; estimate and spec. 1897; ac's and finance: ledgers 1840-1928, parochial ledgers 1837-1927 (gaps), relieving officer's receipt and exp. books 1910-28 (gaps), renewal order book 1917-20, outdoor relief list (abstract) 1913-35, loan ac's book 1875-90, County Council repayments book 1901-20, collector's ledgers 1902-22, 1928-33, financial statements 1920-28, poor rate returns and

Merioneth: Ffestiniog *continued*

memoranda 1877-99; w'h.: master's report and journal 1911-28, clothing and provisions ac's 1843-52, clothing materials and conversion ac's 1901-05, medical journal 1918-21; SAC book 1877-1903; Assessment C'tee min's 1884-1902; treasurer's book (RSA and Glaslyn RDC) 1889-1917; misc. corres. 1865, 1895, 1902-30 (gaps).

Public Record Office, *Kew:*
Corres. etc. 1835-96 [MH 12/16522-41]; staff reg. 1837-1921 [MH 9/7].

Machynlleth [5] (Pennal, Towyn).
See under Montgomeryshire.

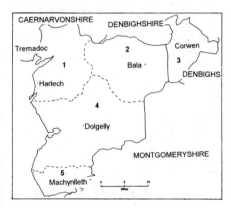

MERIONETH

MONMOUTHSHIRE

(formerly administratively in England).

Unless shown otherwise, records are at
Gwent County Record Office, *Cwmbran.*
Information is based on W.H. Baker, *Guide to the Monmouthshire Record Office,* 1959 (*GMRO*), but including details of subsequent acccessions.

Abergavenny [1].

A. Relief orders 1867-1912; appl. and reports (Blaenavon) 1881; vagrants' outdoor relief lists 1895-1915; orders for adm. to casual ward 1910; school fees: orders 1878-91, receipt and exp. 1878-92; relieving officers' receipt and exp.: Abergavenny 1862-1910, Blaenavon 1870-1910; medical relief lists 1860-1925, and books 1870-71, 1883-90, 1912-19; reg. of successful vac's 1853-69; notices of requirement for vac. etc. 1855, 1868, 1895; MO's case book 1874-82, record of exam's of children 1913-21, inmates 1914-25; weekly returns Form A 1864-1904, 1914-30; births, marriages and deaths reg. 1837-1863 (and quarterly returns 1847-49); notices of marriage 1859-77; reg. of paupers and removal orders 1858-59; rate book (Llanwenarth Ultra) 1866; adm. and discharge reg. 1843-1914; casual paupers reg's: adm. and discharge 1871-1929, cases refused 1877-1933; vagrants adm. and discharge reg. 1870-1, 1890-1906, 1922-23; lodging house casuals 1929-30; school adm. and discharges 1843-84; SAC reg. 1866-85; creed reg. 1868-1911; indoor relief lists 1870-1926; revision reg. of indoor relief 1893-1920; reg. of inmates 1920; reg. of lunatics 1889-94; reg. of mechanical restraint 1890-1928; collectors' receipt and exp. books (various districts) 1890-1910.

B. Min's 1836-1930; C'tee mins: Assessment 1862-88, Boarding-out 1910-30, SAC 1877-1904, RSA 1872-94; corres. 1834-1929; abstract of weekly outdoor relief lists 1866-99; reg. of relief on loan 1877-90; medical returns 1888-1904; sup'an. reg. 1866-1929; SAC officer's reports 1881-84; pauper classification 1857-95; summary of vagrants 1913-22; returns to LGB, numbers and cost of pauper lunatics 1882-86; non-resident and non-settled poor ledgers 1845-72; reg. of contracts 1893; ledgers 1836-1930; treasurer's ledgers 1836-42; parochial ledgers 1848-1928; precepts 1862-91; RSA ledgers 1874-96; various parish overseers' receipt and exp., C19; reg. of securities 1891-1912, 1926-27; overseers' balance sheets 1843-1907 (incomplete); House C'tee reports 1922-25; visitors' books 1869-1913; master's: reports 1870-1928, report and journal 1899-1917, day book 1867-73, journal 1881-1919 (incomplete) and summary 1877-1916; MO's reports 1901-14, report and half yearly statement 1921-29; drug ac's 1867-73; chaplain's book 1840-1917; porter's book 1904-06; labour superin-tendent's receipt and exp. book 1879; ac's of diets and extras 1887, 1901-14; allowance of extras to paupers employed in w'h. 1882-94; wages of servants, sup'an. etc. 1923-25; inventory book 1875-94; inmates' clothing and receipt book 1884-85;

Monmouthshire: Abergavenny *continued*

tradesmen's ac's 1862-72; provision estimates 1880-85; tenders accepted 1912-21; stone ledger 1878-97; w'h. wages and ac's 1919-23.

Public Record Office, Kew:
Corres. etc. 1834-1900 [MH 12/7964-87]; staff reg. 1837-1921 [MH 9/1].

Bedwellty.
A. Appl. and reports (n.d.); relief order books (various districts) 1887-1914; relief order sheets 1914-16, 1928 (No. 3 dist. only); out relief orders 1895-1900, 1919-21; relief order lists 1910-28 (incomplete); abstract of outdoor relief lists 1868-1930 (incomplete); vagrants' outdoor relief lists 1892-1912; relief order books, casual poor 1873-78; non-resident poor relief list c.1900; district medical relief book 1924-26; reg. of non-settled poor 1909-24; reg. of non-resident poor 1908-13; reg's of children under control of Guardians and deserted children c.1900; reg. of young persons (n.d.); reg. of children boarded-out 1910-27, associated pay list 1910-30, receipt and exp. 1910-21; cottage homes revision reg. 1918-27; reg. of appr's (n.d.); reg. of summonses 1907-14; lists of lunatics: annual 1900-09, quarterly 1907-30; vac. reg's: Tredegar 1880-81, Aberystruth and Rock 1896; adm. and discharge reg. (Try-bryn military hospital) 1918-19; creed reg. c.1900; school fees appl. and reports 1886-91.
B. Min's 1849-1930; C'tee min's: Finance 1896-1916, Assessment 1902-08, numerous others 1902-27 (see *GMRO*); declaration of acceptance of office 1907-18; motion book 1903-10; corres. 1870-1930; lists of Guardians and paid officers 1891-1916, 1920-21; legal papers and guarantee bonds (various dates); overseer's receipts and exp. 1912-28; removal officer's notebook 1907-10; settlement notification of chargeability 1908-28; relieving officer's receipt and exp. 1887-1930; weekly and fortnightly returns 1891-1930 various; annual poor rate return 1905-6; reg. of officers and servants c.1890, c.1900; reg. of salaries and deductions 1907-11; ledgers 1849-1930; parochial ledgers 1908-25; non-resident and non-settled poor ledgers 1904-27; treasurer's ledgers 1910-25; salaries ledgers 1911-21, 1929-30; wages book 1911-13; wages receipt book 1927-30; general aggregate orders to treasurer 1924-30; out relief aggregate orders 1924-29; financial statements 1867-1927 (incomplete); tradesmen's ledger 1909-14; reg. of securities 1875-1927; MO's reports, n.d.; super-intendent nurse's reports 1908-11, 1916-24.

Public Record Office, Kew:
Corres. etc. 1848-1900 [MH 12/7992-8023]; staff reg. 1837-1921 [MH 9/2].

Cardiff [6] (Rumney, St. Mellon's).
See under Glamorgan.

Chepstow [7] (partly in Glos.).
A. Relief orders 1910-24; outdoor relief lists: abstracts 1888-1918, vagrants 1915-21; district medical relief: Chepstow 1912-26, Shirenewton 1913-20; vac. reg's 1853-72 (Chepstow District), 1906-18; adm. and discharge reg's 1869-72, 1880-1903, 1909-30 (casuals 1928-37; vagrants 1870-91, 1906-18, 1921-28); tramp book 1898-1902, 1910-13; MO's reports 1922-31; creed reg's 1877-8, 1912-14; indoor relief lists 1870-1930; punishment book 1881-1913; births reg. 1866-1914; valuation lists (by parish) 1899-1929.
B. Min's 1838-1929; C'tee min's: Assessment 1862-69, 1879-1907, (draft) 1924-27, Cottage Homes 1912-23, SAC 1877-1903, RSA 1872-94 and Lydney (Glos.) Parochial 1877-98, Military Service Act 1916 Chepstow Tribunal 1916-18; Guardians attendance 1901-16, officers' bonds 1853-1904 (incomplete); PLB circulars 1867; corres. 1837-1930; out-letters 1873-96; RSA misc. papers 1880-94; boarding-out receipt and exp. 1912-23; relieving officer's receipt and exp. 1910-30 (incomplete); weekly returns: form A 1911-26, form B 1911-28, relieving officer's return of pauperism 1905, 1912-20, births 1879-86; vac. officer's report book 1913-24; service reg. (sup'an.) 1906-29; pauper classification books 1889-1904, 1914-17; calculation books for estimating number of paupers 1911-27; quarterly returns of pauper lunatics 1874-86; stat. statement 1872-93; ledgers 1836-1930; parochial ledgers 1848-1922; non-settled and non-resident poor ledgers 1845-48, 1871-1915; treasurer's books 1907-24; cash book 1915-25; RSA: ledgers (incl. parochial) 1873-94; collector's ledgers 1908-30 (gaps); collector's unpaid rates: Llangwm Ucha 1878-1926, Portskewett 1893-1926, Tidenham (Glos.) 1908-22; collector's monthly statements (by parishes) 1886-1927; overseers' (by parishes): receipt and exp. books 1868-1927 (gaps), balance sheets 1914-26 (gaps); Union contribution calculation books 1911-21; monthly salaries reg. 1924-20; wages receipt book 1918-25; wages book 1925-29; financial statements 1872-1919; RSA financial statements 1874-93; reg. of securities 1877-1929; w'h. visitors' books 1910-30; master's: day book 1910-34 (summary 1908-31), weekly report book 1911-13, report and journal 1913-4, journal and fortnightly report 1917-29, report book 1929-32; diet and extras for sick, lunatics, infants: daily statement 1922, 1924-36 (summary 1925-29), extras ordered (summary) 1929-32; porter's book 1908-18; stone ac's 1898-1910; tobacco and snuff ac's 1911-30; firewood ac's 1911-25; garden and pig ac's 1893-1917; dry tea ac's 1923-30; alcohol book 1901-26; inventory book 1900-1919; contract books 1915-17, 1926-30; wages receipt books 1912-18.

Public Record Office, Kew:
Corres. etc. 1834-1900 [MH 12/8031-56]; staff reg. 1837-1921 [MH 9/4].

Dore [2] (Grosmont, Llangua).
See under Herefordshire.

Monmouthshire *continued*

Monmouth [3] (partly in Glos.).
A. Relief order books 1910-30 (gaps), abstracts 1904-17; DMO's relief book 1915-23; MO's children's exam. book 1914-19; reg. of non-resident poor 1887-95, 1905-11; reg. of children boarded-out 1906-21; reg. of deserted children 1889; reg. of infants 1904-28; reg. of persons undertaking nursing and maintenance of infants, n.d.; reg. of lunatics in w'h. 1892-1909, in Asylum 1882-1916; adm. and discharge reg's 1853-1926 (missing 1859, 1894-97) (casual paupers 1899-1931); medical relief books 1897-1914; inmates exam. book 1914-29; creed reg's 1881-1930; births and deaths reg's 1866-1914; indoor relief list and abstract 1971-2, 1894-1930; punishment books 1859-1930; reg. of visits to boys and girls 1897.
B. Min's 1839-41, 1847-49, 1857-1930; C'tee min's: Assessment 1888-1927, Children's Homes 1921-30, SAC 1877-1904, Joint Vagrancy 1913-30; Guardians' declarations 1894-1928, attendance 1925-30; corres. from government departments 1911-16; letter books 1869-1924; treasurer's letter book 1868-74; general corres. 1836-1930; boarded-out maintenance pay list 1915-30; boarding-out receipt and exp. 1910-1; relieving officers receipts and exp. 1910-16; weekly returns: form A 1883-1930, form B 1904-5; pauper classification book 1869-1912; staff reg. 1897-1911, 1924-30; housing inspection A1 reg. 1911-14; ledgers 1837-1930 (missing 1850); parochial ledgers 1836-41, 1854-62, 1866-71, 1876-1927; treasurer's ac's of receipts and exp. 1914-27, 1929-30; balance book 1921-28; collector's: ledgers 1927, monthly statement 1923-27, receipt and exp. 1906-22; overseers' receipt and exp. (by parishes) 1892-1927 (gaps); reg's of County Council repayments: lunacy 1889-1915, registrars 1890-1929, officers' salaries 1892-1928; reg's: officers' salaries 1907-22. monthly salaries 1925-28, cheques issued 1928-30; financial statements 1900-22; House C'tee report books 1914-21, 1925-30; visitors book 1899-1918 (gaps); lady visitors book 1895-1931; master's: day book 1891-2, 1898-1931 (summary 1897-1929), reports 1899-1916, 1923-30, half yearly reports 1920-23, 1927-31, receipts and exp. 1904-07, 1911-15; matron's reports to House C'tee 1915-27; MO's reports 1901-28; chaplain's reports 1898-1932; officiating Free Church ministers' record 1913-31; porter's book 1900-08, 1910-29; diet and extras: daily list 1929-32, daily and weekly summary 1914-19, ac's 1901-03, tea. sugar and milk ac's 1894-1917; inventory book 1888-1904; stone stock ac's 1876-1903; garden and pig ac's 1882-1931; oakum receipt and sale ac's 1899-1915; wood receipt and sale ac's 1891-1923; alcohol book 1901-06.

Gloucestershire Record Office, Gloucester.
A. Poor rate books: Coleford, Newland, Staunton and West Dean 1873, 1914-26; valuation lists: West Dean 1921.

Public Record Office, Kew:
Corres. etc. 1834-1900 [MH 12/8059-82]; staff reg. 1837-1921 [MH 9/11].

Newport [5] (partly in Glamorgan).
A. Relief order books 1912-28 (gaps), abstract 1905-10, 1926-28; school fees appl. and report book 1880-1; appr. indentures 1851-91; boarded-out relief lists 1909-23; summary of removal cases to be enquired into by removal officer 1889-98; relieving officers' reg. of notifications of tuberculosis appl. and report books 1909-13; DMOs' relief books (by district) 1881-1930; reg's: children under control of Guardians 1893-1913, boarded-out children 1910-12, children sent to certified houses 1896-1911, persons receiving infants 1909-17, persons in institutions 1900-25, removals and settlements 1897-1914, appr's 1845-95; Caerleon Industrial Schools: adm. and discharge reg's 1866-87, 1897-1902, MO's report book 1895-99, medical relief books 1898-1902, deaths reg. 1867-1901, creed reg. 1887-1902, indoor relief list 1896-1902, children's reg., n.d., reg. of young persons 1865-1901, under 16 hired from Caerleon School 1865-79, taken as servants from w'h. 1908-12; Workhouse: adm. and discharge reg's 1837-1950, births reg's 1837-1925, deaths reg. 1837-1914, 1924-49; reg. of operations 1926-44; notification of tuberculosis by MO 1913-15; creed reg. 1894-1927; indoor relief lists 1906-48; outdoor relief list 1900, 1903, 1908-26; reg. of mechanical restraint 1928-47.
B. Min's 1836-1927; agendas 1879-80, 1885-1930; C'tee min's: Caerleon Schools 1859-1905, Finance 1842-1930, Nuisances 1848-56, RSA 1872-94, SAC 1877-94, numerous others 1872-1930 (see *GMRO*; Guardians: signatures 1894-1927, voting record 1919; c'tee signatures 1895-1926; LGB election order book 1894-97; LGB orders book 1836-45; letter books 1936-58; corres. etc. 1836-1930; relief on loan lists 1926-28; settlement and removal officer's diary 1902-12, 1924-29; relieving officer's: receipts and exp. (by district) 1908-30 (gaps), voucher lists 1921, 1929-30, receipts, extra Christmas relief on loan, n.d.; weekly return form A 1890-1929; pauper classification 1892-94; calculation book for ascertaining number of paupers 1912-14; school attendance officer's reports 1877-87; return of attendance at elementary schools 1899-1904; drug stock reg., Queen's Hill (Newport) Dispensary 1900-26; annual poor rate return 1899; Rumney parochial terrier 1893; Sup'an. reg., n.d.; ledgers 1836-1925; parochial ledgers 1850-1927; treasurer's ac's 1909-25; RSA: ledgers 1873-94, treasurer's book 1873-78, receipt and exp. 1893-95; SAC ledger 1878-81; collector's: ledgers 1904-08, monthly statements (par. Bettwys) 1881-92; precepts 1920-29; overseers' receipts and exp. (by parishes) 1904-26; reg. of orders on relatives to maintain 1925-6; out-relief ledger 1921; financial statements 1900-21; Caerleon Industrial School: Master's: weekly report and journal 1869-83, day book and quarterly summary 1897-1902, summary 1888-1902, receipts and exp. 1880-1902; ac's 1895-97;

chaplain's reports 1878-1902; porter's book 1901-2, 1908-10, 1927-36; dietaries 1869-74; provisions ac's 1900-02; necessaries and misc. ac's 1900-02; receiving wards book 1896-1902; reg. of ag'mts with employers 1897-1913; visitors book 1860-1902; children's visitors books 1896-1902; clothing ac's 1898-1902; farm ac's 1890-92, inventory books 1900, 1929; reg. of school exam. results 1897-1902; misc. corres. and reports 1896-98; Workhouse: inventory books 1905-19, 1929-47, bedding and linen 1908-39; outdoor boots reg. 1925-38; goods receipts 1923-27.

Public Record Office, *Kew:*
Corres. etc. 1834-1900 [MH 12/8086-140]; staff reg. 1837-1921 [MH 9/12].

Pontypool [4].

A. Relief order books (by districts) 1878-80, 1892-1930 (gaps), abstracts 1900-18 (gaps); boarding-out relief list 1908-12; district medical relief books 1906-24 (gaps); monthly list of births 1871-88; reg's of successful vac's 1857-71; vac. reg's 1907-22; returns of births (Usk) 1889-1910; reg's: infants c.1906-23, children under control of Guardians 1901-16, boarded-out children c.1896-1909, persons notifying retention or receipt of infant 1898-9, 1917-26, persons undertaking nursing of infants for reward c.1914, notices of servants and appr's received from other Unions c.1896, children sent to training homes n.d., persons chargeable c.1920; adm. and discharge reg's 1858-1930 (gaps) (vagrants 1892-1925 (summary 1896-1914); casuals 1925-30, school 1863-1901); w'h. school attendance book (girls) 1868-72; MO's: record books 1914-30, exam. book 1899-1901, 1914-23; reg. of medical exam. of infants and children 1914-27; medical relief books 1884-1925; notices of births 1913-30; deaths reg's 1869-94; creed reg's 1873-1914; indoor relief order books 1868-1930 (abstract 1911-30); reg. of lunatics 1890-1914; punishment book 1852-1912; reg. of mechanical restraint 1901-28; outdoor labour book 1907; bathing reg. 1920-29.

B. Min's 1836-45, 1854-1930; Guardians attendance 1878-1902, 1906-30, signatures 1921-30; SAC min's 1877-1904; other c'tee min's 1884-1930 (see GMRO); Guardians declarations 1895-1928; PLB orders 1864-69; out letters 1873-1912 (Joint Vagrancy C'tee 1917-22); misc. corres. 1842-1929; school fees order book, n.d.; boarding-out receipts and exp. 1906-25; relieving officers' receipts and exp. 1883-1922 (gaps); weekly returns: form A 1893-1930, form B 1911-30; pauper classification 1872-74, 1911-14; returns of infants' deaths 1871-83, 1893-1915; inspector of nuisances reports 1909-12; lunacy cert. book 1873-83; sup'an. reg's 1899-1930; ledgers 1836-45, 1847, 1852-1918, 1929-30; parochial ledgers 1872-1910; non-resident and non-settled poor ledger 1859-1911; treasurer's ac's 1907-27; relief schemes ac's 1927-8; RSA ledgers 1874-94, parochial ledgers 1874-95; collectors' ac's 1872-1926 (gaps), monthly statements 1893-1927

(gaps), report books 1901-29; overseers' receipts and exps., balance sheets 1868-1927 (gaps); misc. valuations of industrial hereditaments 1927-8; financial statements 1886-1926; reg. of securities 1870-1930; analytical reg. of vagrants, n.d., c.1930; visitors books 1862-1930, ladies 1893-1906; visitors weekly payment book 1912-28; master's: day book 1868-9, 1875-79, 1885-90, 1898-1910, 1913-26 (summary 1901-31), report and journal 1876-1914, report book 1880-84, journals 1893-1923 (gaps), weekly reports 1896-1912, journal and fortnightly reports 1920-29; MO's reports 1892-1928; chaplain's reports 1847-1913 (gaps); porter's book 1916-7; district officers' report on adm's to w'h. and infirmary 1903-12 (gaps); inventory books 1848-62, 1910; stone ac's 1881-89, 1901-12; tobacco and snuff ac's 1894-1928; master's garden books 1883-1930, firewood book 1886-1930; oakum ac's 1906-15; extra tea, sugar and milk ac's 1897-1925; pauper service book 1869-1908; school attendance books 1870-1902 (gaps).

Public Record Office, *Kew:*
Corres. etc. 1834-1900 [MH 12/8152-80]; staff reg. 1837-1921 [MH 9/13].

Joint Vagrancy Committee (Brecknock, Glamorgan and Monmouthshire).
B. Min's 1913-30; ledger 1923-48.

Unidentified Unions.
B. Diet and extras daily statement 1914-26 (gaps).

Joint Poor Law Establishment Committee.
B. Min's 1913-4; corres. 1913-15.

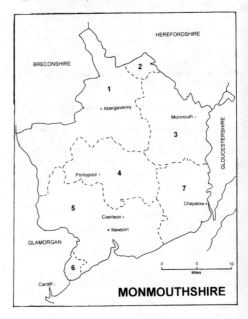

MONMOUTHSHIRE

MONTGOMERYSHIRE

Unless shown otherwise, records are at *Powys Record Office, Llandrindod Wells.*

Atcham [5] (Cruggion).
See under Shropshire.

Clun [6] (Hyssington, Snead).
See under Shropshire.

Dolgellau/Dolgelly [1] (Mallwyd).
See under Merioneth.

Forden [7] (later **Montgomery and [Welsh]Pool**).
A. Welshpool parish rate book 1926.
B. Special C'tee min's 1818-25; officer's report book 1795-98; lists of Guardians etc. 1928-9.
Public Record Office, Kew:
Corres. etc. 1846-1896 [MH 12/16580-96]; staff reg. 1837-1921 [MH 9/7].

Llanfyllin [2] (partly in Denbighs.).
A. Case papers c.1909-30; boarded-out children file c.1911-14; reg. of inmates 1885-1974; births reg. 1914-41; cases 1906-48; deaths reg. 1914-72; creed reg's 1909-39; SAC min's 1877-1904.
B. Min's 1902-08, 1911-23; ledgers 1837-87; treasurer's ac's 1914-22; parochial ledgers 1861-66, 1903-22; letters to clerk 1871-73; w'h. rules, n.d.
Public Record Office, Kew:
Corres. etc. 1834-1896 [MH 12/16543-63]; staff reg. 1837-1921 [MH 9/10].

Llanidloes see **Newtown**.

Machynlleth [3] (partly in Merioneth, Cardigans.).
No locally held records known.
Public Record Office, Kew:
Corres. etc. 1836-1896 [MH 12/16564-77]; staff reg. 1837-1921 [MH 9/11].

Montgomery and [Welsh]Pool see **Forden**.

Newtown and Llanidloes [4].
See B. Owen, 'The Newtown and Llanidloes Poor Law Union Workhouse, Caersws, 1837-1847', *Montgomeryshire Coll.* **78** (1990).
No locally held records known.
Public Record Office, Kew:
Corres. etc. 1834-1896 [MH 12/16597-617]; staff reg. 1837-1921 [MH 9/12].

Pool or **Welshpool** see **Forden**.

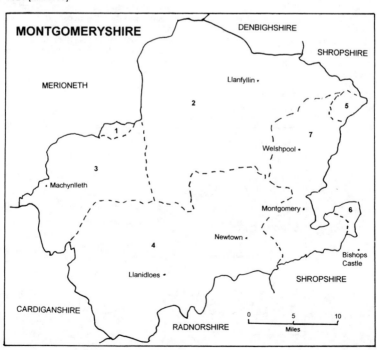

PEMBROKESHIRE

See R. Davies, 'Poor Law Board correspondence (1834-1909)', *Dyfed F.H.J.* **4.**2 (1991) (from PRO MH 12 records, referring to Cards. and Pembs.).

Unless shown otherwise, records are at *Pembrokeshire Record Office (Dyfed Archive Service), Haverfordwest.*

Cardigan [1] (Bayvil, Bridell, Cilgerran, Dinas, St. Dogmel's, Eglwyserw, Llanfair Nant gwyn, Llanfihangel Penbedw, Llantwyd, Llanychlwydog, Maenordewi, Melinau, Monnington or Eglwys Wythiel, Molygrove or Trewyddel, Nevern, Newport, Whitchurch or Eglwyswen).
See under Cardiganshire.

Haverfordwest [2].
A. Adm. and discharge 1879-1950 (gaps); births and deaths reg's 1866-1949; reg. of inmates c.1920-48; reg. of mechanical restraint 1890; punishment book 1898-1947; creed reg. c.1922-42; various adm. and discharge cert's of soldiers 1872/3; abstract of outdoor relief lists 1919-30; reg. of lunatics in asylum c.1890-1930; reg. of appr's 1896-1911; reg. of boarded-out children 1889-1927; collector's receipt and exp. book (St. David's) 1909-34.
B. Min's 1837-42, 1845-1930; C'tee min's: W'h. 1837-62, Assessment 1862-1927, House 1907-44, Boarding-out 1910-26, Liability of relatives 1912-14; MO's contracts 1883-1908; dietary 1917; letter from LGB 1895; various plans c.1837, 1869, 1882; receipts and exp. book (St. Martin) 1836-48; poor rate returns 1891-1929; ledger 1928-32; parochial ledger 1913-15; reg. of officers' appointments 1895-1929; treasurer's ac's ledger 1927-32; letter book 1876-78; misc. files ; corres. files (c.1900-30, subject to 100 year closure).
Public Record Office, Kew:
Corres. etc. 1834-96 [MH 12/16619-49]; staff reg. 1837-1921 [MH 9/8].

Narberth [4] (partly in Carmarthens.).
A. Rate books 1910-15 (poor condition); relief order books (100 year restriction): Narberth 1918-25, Slebech 1919-28, Llanboidy 1921-30;
B. Min's 1837-1947 (gaps); Assessment C'tee min's 1920-27; letter books 1869-1923 (gaps); RSA letter book 1884-92; deeds 1838, 1840; c'tee reports: House 1914-22, others 1921-34; ledger 1898-1900, 1929-31; parochial ledger 1925-27; public assistance ledger 1927-31; cash books 1923-32; treasurer's receipts and exp. book 1925-29; estimates and precepts calculations 1917-22; misc. files 1845-1927.
Public Record Office, Kew:
Corres. etc. 1834-96 [MH 12/16652-66]; staff reg. 1837-1921 [MH 9/12].

Newcastle in Emlyn [3] (Cilrhedyn, Clyde, Llanfrynach, Penrydd).
See under Cardiganshire.

Pembroke [5].
A. Creed reg's 1869-1902; adm. and discharge book 1912-15; reg. of inmates c.1905-55; inmates' property reg. 1915-48; reg. of births in hospital 1914-47; reg. of births in w'h. 1866-1913; reg. of deaths in w'h. 1837-66; cert's to detain lunatics 1894-1920.
B. Min's 1839-1928 (gaps); C'tee min's: Assessment 1862-88, Children's Homes 1915-21, Children's Homes, Boarding out and Finance (sic) 1912-30, House 1923-28, Finance and Relatives' arrears 1925-39; letter books 1837-52; exp. for children boarded-out 1925-40; unemployment relief ac's 1926-29; cash book 1929-32; w'h. plans 1837; misc. files incl. PLC orders, leases, etc. (and photographs etc. of Riverside).
Public Record Office, Kew:
Corres. etc. 1834-96 [MH 12/16667-86]; staff reg. 1837-1921 [MH 9/13].

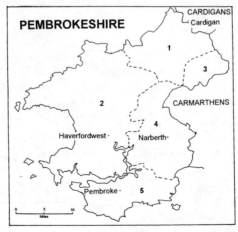

RADNORSHIRE

Unless shown otherwise, records are at
Powys Record Office, Llandrindod Wells.

Builth [4] (Aberedeu, Bettwys Disserth, Creguna,
Disserth and Trecoed, Llanbadarn y Garreg,
Llandrindod, Llanelwedd, Llanfaredd, Llansaintfraed
in Elvel, Rhulen).
See under Brecknock.

Hay [6] (Boughrood, Bryngwyn, (Bettws) Clyro,
Glasbury, Llanbedr, Llandeilo Graban, Llandewi,
Llanstephen, Llowes, Painscastle).
See under Brecknock.

Kington [5] (Colva, Gladestry, Glascomb,
Llandeglay, Llanfihangel Nant Melor, Michaelchurch
upon Arrow, Newchurch, New and Old Radnor).
See under Herefordshire.

Knighton [2] (partly in Herefs., Shrops.).
A. List of paupers 1838; appl. and report books
1918-20; out relief lists 1917-41; receipts and exp.
books 1905-6, 1918-9; marriage notice book
(Knighton) 1841-83; Knighton parish rate books
1911-29.
B. Min's 1901-30; ledgers 1922-30; treasurer's ac's
1924-30; returns of paupers 1924-26; plans etc. late
C19 - early C20; visitors' exp. book 1920-29; rates
papers 1902-27; census plans (Llanbister) 1911,
1921; vac. officer's report book 1907-14; reg's of
officers 1897-1924.
Public Record Office, Kew:
Corres. etc. 1834-96 [MH 12/16690-707]; staff reg.
1837-1921 [MH 9/9].

Presteigne [3] (partly in Herefs.).
A. Marriage notice book (Presteigne and Knighton)
1841-77.
Public Record Office, Kew:
Corres. etc. 1836-81 [MH 12/16709-14]; staff reg.
1837-1921 [MH 9/13].

Rhayader [1] (partly in Brecknock).
A. Collector's receipt and exp. books 1917-48.
B. Min's 1836-89, 1904-20; ledgers 1902-30;
collector's ledger (Nantmel) 1914-30; vac. officer's
report books 1912-37; RSA min's 1872-98.
Public Record Office, Kew:
Corres. etc. 1834-96 (missing 1854-57) [MH 12/
16715-26]; staff reg. 1837-1921 [MH 9/14].

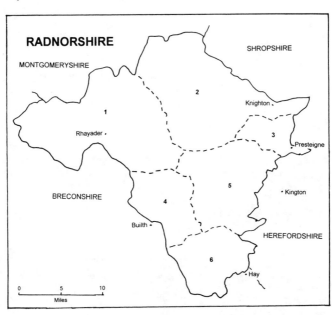

ALPHABETICAL LISTING OF UNIONS

Aberaeron, *Cards.*
Abergavenny, *Mon.*
Aberystwyth, *Cards.*
Abingdon, *Berks.*
Albans, St., *Herts.*
Alcester, *Warw.*
Alderbury, *Wilts.*
Alstonfield, *Staffs.*
Alnwick, *Nhmbd.*
Alresford, *Hants.*
Alston, *Cumbs.*
Alton, *Hants.*
Altrincham, *Ches.*
Alverstoke, *Hants.*
Amersham, *Bucks.*
Amesbury, *Wilts.*
Ampthill, *Beds.*
Andover, *Hants.*
Anglesey, *Ang.*
Arrington, *Cambs.*
Arundel, *Sussex*
Asaph, St., *Flints.*
Ash, *Surrey*
Ashbourne, *Dbys.*
Ashby de la Zouch, *Leics.*
Ashford, East, *Kent*
Ashford, West, *Kent*
Ashton, Long, *Som.*
Ashton under Lyne, *Lancs.*
Aston, *Warw.*
Atcham, *Salop.*
Atherstone, *Warw.*
Auckland (Bishop's), *Durh.*
Austell, St., *Corn.*
Axbridge, *Som.*
Axminster, *Devon*
Aylesbury, *Bucks.*
Aylesford, North, *Kent*
Aylsham, *Norf.*
Aysgarth, *Yorks. N.R.*

Bainbridge, *Yorks. N.R.*
Bakewell, *Dbys.*
Bala, *Merioneth*
Banbury, *Oxon.*
Bangor, *Caerns.*
Barnet, *Herts.*
Barnsley, *Yorks. W.R.*
Barnstaple, *Devon*
Barrow in Furness, *Lancs.*
Barton Regis, *Glos.*
Barton upon Irwell, *Lancs.*

Barwick(-in-Elmet), *Yorks. W.R.*
Basford, *Notts.*
Basingstoke, *Hants.*
Bath, *Som.*
Battle, *Sussex*
Beaminster, *Dorset*
Beaumaris, *Caerns.*
Bedale, *Yorks. N.R.*
Bedford, *Beds.*
Bedwelty, *Mon.*
Belford, *Nhmbd.*
Bellingham, *Nhmbd.*
Belper, *Dbys.*
Berkhampstead, *Herts.*
Bermondsey, *London: Surrey*
Berwick-on-Tweed, *Nhmbd.*
Bethnal Green, *London: Middx.*
Beverley, *Yorks. E.R.*
Bicester, *Oxon.*
Bideford, *Devon*
Bierley, North, *Yorks. W.R.*
Biggleswade, *Beds.*
Billericay, *Essex*
Billesden, *Leics.*
Bingham, *Notts.*
Birkenhead, *Ches.*
Birmingham, *Warw.*
Bishops Auckland, *Dur.*
Bishops Stortford, *Herts.*
Blaby, *Leics.*
Blackburn, *Lancs.*
Blandford, *Dorset*
Blean, *Kent*
Blofield, *Norf.*
Blything, *Suff.*
Bodmin, *Corn.*
Bolton, *Lancs.*
Bootle, *Cumbd.*
Bosmere, *Suff.*
Bosworth, Market, *Leics.*
Boston, *Lincs.*
Boughton, Great, *Ches.*
Bourne, *Lincs.*
Bournemouth, *Hants.*
Brackley, *N'hants.*
Bradfield, *Berks.*
Bradford(-on-Avon), *Wilts.*
Bradford, *Yorks. W.R.*
Braintree, *Essex*
Bramley, *Yorks. W.R.*

Brampton, *Cumbd.*
Brecknock, *Brecons.*
Brentford, *Middx.*
Bridge, *Kent*
Bridgend, *Glam.*
Bridgewater, *Som.*
Bridgnorth, *Salop.*
Bridlington, *Yorks. E.R.*
Bridport, *Dorset*
Brighton, *Sussex,*
Brinton, *Norf.*
Bristol, *Glos.*
Brixworth, *N'hants.*
Bromley, *Kent*
Bromsgrove, *Worcs.*
Bromwich, West, *Staffs.*
Bromyard, *Heref.*
Buckingham, *Bucks.*
Bucklow, *Ches.*
Builth, *Brecons.*
Buntingford, *Herts.*
Burnley, *Lancs.*
Burslem, *Staffs.*
Burton-on-Trent, *Staffs.*
Bury, *Lancs.*
Bury St. Edmunds, *Suff.*

Caernarvon, *Caerns.*
Caistor, *Lincs.*
Calne, *Wilts.*
Camberwell, *London: Surrey*
Cambridge, *Cambs.*
Camelford, *Corn.*
Cannock, *Staffs.*
Canterbury, *Kent*
Cardiff, *Glam.*
Cardigan, *Cards.*
Carlisle, *Cumbd.,*
Carlton, *Yorks. W.R.*
Carmarthen, *Carms.*
Carnarvon, *Caerns.*
Castle Ward, *Nhmbd.*
Catherington, *Hants.*
Caton, *Lancs.*
Caxton, *Cambs.*
Cerne, *Dorset*
Chailey, *Sussex*
Chapel en le Frith, *Dbys.*
Chard, *Som.*
Cheadle, *Staffs.*
Chelmsford, *Essex*
Chelsea, *London: Middx.*
Cheltenham, *Glos.*
Chepstow, *Mon.*
Chertsey, *Surrey*

Chester, *Ches.*
Chesterfield, *Dbys.*
Chester-le-Street, *Dur.*
Chesterton, *Cambs.*
Chichester, *Sussex*
Chippenham, *Wilts.*
Chipping Norton, *Oxon.*
Chipping Sodbury, *Glos.*
Chorley, *Lancs.*
Chorlton, *Lancs.*
Christchurch, *Hants.*
Church Stretton, *Salop.*
Cirencester, *Glos.*
Clapham, *London: Surrey*
Clavering, *Norf.*
Claydon, *Suff.*
Cleobury Mortimer, *Salop.*
Clerkenwell, *London: Middx.*
Clifton, *Glos.*
Clitheroe, *Lancs.*
Clun, *Salop.*
Clutton, *Som.*
Cockermouth, *Cumbd.*
Colchester, *Essex*
Columb, St. Major, *Corn.*
Congleton, *Ches.*
Conway, *Caerns.*
Cookham, *Berks.*
Corwen, *Merioneth*
Cosford, *Suff.*
Coventry, *Warw.*
Cowbridge, *Glam.*
Cranborne, *Dorset*
Cranbrook, *Kent*
Crediton, *Devon*
Crickhowell, *Brecons.*
Cricklade, *Wilts.*
Croydon, *Surrey*
Cuckfield, *Sussex*

Darlington, *Dur.*
Dartford, *Kent*
Daventry, *N'hants.*
Depwade, *Norf.*
Derby, *Dbys.*
Derby, West, *Lancs.*
Devizes, *Wilts.*
Devonport, *Devon*
Dewsbury, *Yorks. W.R.*
Docking, *Norf.*
Dolgelly, *Merioneth*
Doncaster, *Yorks. W.R.* .
Dorchester, *Dorset*

Dore, *Heref.*
Dorking, *Surrey*
Dover, *Kent*
Downham, *Norf.*
Drayton, *Salop.*
Driffield, *Yorks. E.R.*
Droitwich, *Worcs.*
Droxford, *Hants.*
Dudley, *Staffs.*
Dulverton, *Som.*
Dunmow, *Essex*
Durham, *Dur.*
Dursley, *Glos.*

Easington, *Dur.*
Easingwold, *Yorks. N.R.*
Eastbourne, *Sussex*
East Ashford, *Kent*
East Flegg, *Norf.*
East Grinstead, *Sussex*
Easthampstead, *Brks.*
East Preston, *Sussex*
East Retford, *Notts.*
Eastry, *Kent*
East Stonehouse,
  Devon
East Ward, *Westmd.*
Ecclesall Bierlow,
  Yorks. W.R.
Edmonton, *Middx.*
Elham, *Kent*
Ellesmere, *Salop.*
Ely, *Cambs.*
Epping, *Essex*
Epsom, *Surrey*
Erpingham, *Norf.*
Eton, *Bucks.*
Evesham, *Worcs.*
Exeter, *Devon*

Faith, St., *Norf.*
Falmouth, *Corn.*
Fareham, *Hants.*
Farnborough, *Hants.*
Farnham, *Surrey*
Faringdon, *Berks.*
Faversham, *Kent*
Festiniog, *Merioneth*
Firle, West, *Sussex*
Flegg, East and West,
  Norf.
Foleshill, *Warw.*
Forden, *Mont.*
Fordingbridge, *Hants.*
Forehoe, *Norf.*
Forest, New, *Hants.*
Freebridge Lynn, *Norf.*
Frome, *Som.*
Fulham, *London: Middx.*
Fylde, The, *Lancs.*

Gainsborough, *Lincs.*
Garrigill, *Cumbd.*
Garstang, *Lancs.*
Gateshead, *Dur.*
George, St., Blooms-
  bury, *London: Middx.*
George, St., Hanover
  Sq., *London: Middx.*
George, St., in the East,
  London: Middx.
George, St., Southwark,
  London: Surrey
Germans, St., *Corn.*
Giles, St., Bloomsbury,
  London: Middx.
Glandford Brigg, *Lincs.*
Glendale, *Nhmbd.*
Glossop, *Dbys.*
Gloucester, *Glos.*
Godstone, *Surrey*
Goole, *Yorks. W.R.*
Gower, *Glam.*
Grantham, *Lincs.*
Gravesend, *Kent*
Great Broughton, *Ches.*
Greenwich, *London:*
  Kent
Grimsby, *Lincs.*
Grinstead, East, *Sussex*
Guildford, *Surrey*
Guiltcross, *Norf.*
Guisborough, *Yorks.*
  N.R.

Hackney, *London:*
  Middx.
Hailsham, *Sussex*
Halifax, *Yorks. W.R.*
Halstead, *Essex*
Haltwhistle, *Nhmbd.*
Ham, West, *Essex*
Hambledon, *Surrey*
Hampstead, *London:*
  Middx.
Harborough, Market,
  Leics.
Hardingstone, *N'hants.*
Hartismere, *Suff.*
Hartlepool, *Dur.*
Hartney Wintney,
  Hants.
Haslingden, *Lancs.*
Hastings, *Sussex*
Hatfield, *Herts.*
Havant, *Hants.*
Haverfordwest, *Pembs.*
Hawarden, *Flints.*
Hay, *Brecons.*
Hayfield, *Dbys.*
Headington, *Oxon.*
Headley, *Hants.*
Helmsley, *Yorks. N.R.*

Helston, *Corn.*
Hemel Hempstead,
  Herts.
Hemsworth, *Yorks.*
  W.R.
Hendon, *Middx.*
Henley, *Oxon.*
Henstead, *Norf.*
Hereford, *Heref.*
Hertford, *Herts.*
Hexham, *Nhmbd.*
Highworth, *Wilts.*
Hinckley, *Leics.*
Hitchin, *Herts.*
Holbeach, *Lincs.*
Holbeck, *Yorks. W.R.*
Holborn, *London:*
  Middx.
Hollingbourn, *Kent*
Holsworthy, *Devon*
Holyhead, *Ang.*
Holywell, *Flints.*
Honiton, *Devon*
Hoo, *Kent*
Horncastle, *Lincs.*
Horsham, *Sussex*
Houghton le Spring,
  Dur.
Howden, *Yorks. E.R.*
Hoxne, *Suff.*
Huddersfield, *Yorks.*
  W.R.
Hull, *Yorks E.R.*
Hungerford, *Berks.*
Hunslet, *Yorks. W.R.*
Huntingdon, *Hunts.*
Hursley, *Hants.*

Ipswich, *Suff.*
Islington, *London:*
  Middx.
Ives, St., *Hunts.*

James, St., Westmin-
  ster, *London: Middx.*

Keighley, *Yorks. W.R.*
Kendal, *Westmd.*
Kensington, *London:*
  Middx.
Kettering, *N'hants.*
Keynsham,, *Som.*
Kidderminster, *Worcs.*
Kingsbridge, *Devon*
Kingsclere, *Hants.*
Kings Lynn, *Norf.*
Kings Norton, *Worcs.*
Kingston-on-Hull,
  Yorks. E.R.
Kingston-on-Thames,
  Surrey
Kington, *Heref.*

Kirkby Moorside, *Yorks.*
  N.R.
Knaresborough, *Yorks.*
  W.R.
Knighton, *Radnors.*

Lambeth, *London:*
  Surrey
Lampeter, *Cards.*
Lancaster, *Lancs.*
Lanchester, *Dur.*
Langport, *Som.*
Launceston, *Corn.*
Launditch, *Norf.*
Ledbury, *Heref.*
Leeds, *Yorks. W.R.*
Leek, *Staffs.*
Leicester, *Leics.*
Leigh, *Lancs.*
Leighton Buzzard,
  Beds.
Leominster, *Heref.*
Lewes, *Sussex*
Lewisham, *London:*
  Kent
Lexden, *Essex*
Leyburn, *Yorks. N.R.*
Lichfield, *Staffs.*
Lincoln, *Lincs.*
Linton, *Cambs,*
Liskeard, *Corn.*
Liverpool, *Lancs.*
Llandilo Fawr, *Carms.*
Llandovery, *Carms.*
Llanelly, *Carms.*
Llanfyllin, *Mont.*
Llanrwst, *Denbs.*
Loddon, *Norf.*
London, City, *London:*
  Middx.
London, East, *London:*
  Middx.
London, West, *London:*
  Middx.
Long Ashton, *Som.*
Lynn, Freebridge, *Norf.*
Lynn, Kings, *Norf.*

Macclesfield, *Ches.*
Machynlleth, *Mont.*
Madeley, *Salop.*
Maidenhead, *Berks.*
Maidstone, *Kent,*
Maldon, *Kent*
Malling, *Kent*
Malmesbury, *Wilts.*
Malton, *Yorks. N.R.*
Manchester, *Lancs.*
Manchester, South,
  Lancs.
Mansfield, *Notts.*

Margaret, St., Westminster, *London: Middx.*
Market Bosworth, *Leics.*
Market Harborough, *Leics.*
Marlborough, *Wilts.*
Martin, St., in the Fields, *London: Mdx.*
Martley, *Worcs.*
Marylebone, St., *London: Middx.*
Medway, *Kent*
Melksham, *Wilts.*
Melton Mowbray, *Leics.*
Mere, *Wilts.*
Meriden, *Warw.*
Merthyr Tydfil, *Glam.*
Middlesbrough, *Yorks. N.R.*
Midhurst, *Sussex*
Mildenhall, *Suff.*
Mile End Old Town, *London: Middx.*
Milton, *Kent*
Mitford, *Norfolk*
Molton, South, *Devon*
Monmouth, *Mon.*
Montgomery, *Mont.*
Morpeth, *Nhmbd.*
Mutford, *Suff.*

Nantwich, *Ches.*
Narberth, *Pembs.*
Neath, *Glam.*
Neots, St., *Hunts.*
Newark, *Notts.*
Newbury, *Berks.*
Newcastle in Emlyn, *Carms.*
Newcastle under Lyme, *Staffs.*
Newcastle on Tyne, *Nhmbd.*
Newent, *Glos.*
New Forest, *Hants.*
Newhaven, *Sussex*
Newington St. Mary, *London: Surrey*
Newmarket, *Cambs. and Suff.*
Newport, *Mon.*
Newport, *Salop.*
Newport Pagnell, *Bucks.*
Newton Abbot, *Devon*
Newtown, *Mont.*
Northallerton, *Yorks. N.R.*
Northampton, *N'hants.*
North Aylesford, *Kent*
North Bierley, *Yorks. W.R.*

Northleach, *Glos.*
Northwich, *Ches.*
North Witchford, *Cambs.*
Norton, Chipping, *Oxon.*
Norton, Kings, *Worcs.*
Norwich, *Norf.*
Nottingham, *Notts.*
Nuneaton, *Warw.*

Oakham, *Rutland*
Okehampton, *Devon*
Olave, St., *London: Surrey*
Oldham, *Lancs.*
Ongar, *Essex*
Ormskirk, *Lancs.*
Orsett, *Essex*
Oswestry, *Salop.*
Otley, *Yorks. W.R.*
Oundle, *N'hants.*
Ouseburn, Great, *Yorks. W.R.*
Oxford, *Oxon.*

Paddington, *London: Middx.*
Pancras, St., *London: Middx.*
Pateley Bridge, *Yorks. W.R.*
Patrington, *Yorks. E.R.*
Pembroke, *Pembs.*
Penistone, *Yorks. W.R.*
Penkridge, *Staffs.*
Penrith, *Cumbd.*
Penzance, *Corn.*
Pershore, *Worcs.*
Peterborough, *N'hants.*
Petersfield, *Hants.*
Petworth, *Sussex*
Pewsey, *Wilts.*
Pickering, *Yorks. N.R.*
Plomesgate, *Suff.*
Plymouth, *Devon*
Plympton St. Mary, *Devon*
Pocklington, *Yorks. E.R.*
Pontardewe, *Glam.*
Pontefract, *Yorks. W.R.*
Pontypool, *Mon.*
Pontypridd, *Glam.*
Pool, *Mont.*
Poole, *Dorset*
Poplar, *London: Middx.*
Portsea Island, *Hants.*
Portsmouth, *Hants.*
Potterspury, *N'hants.*
Prescot, *Lancs.*
Presteigne, *Radnors.*
Preston, *Lancs.*

Preston, East, *Sussex*
Preston, Great, *Yorks. W.R.*
Prestwich, *Lancs.*
Purbeck, *Dorset*
Pwllheli, *Caerns.*

Radford, *Notts.*
Ramsbury, *Berks.*
Reading, *Berks.*
Redruth, *Corn.*
Reeth, *Yorks. N.R.*
Reigate, *Surrey*
Retford, East, *Notts.*
Rhayader, *Radnors.*
Richmond, *Surrey*
Richmond, *Yorks. N.R.*
Ringwood, *Hants.*
Ripon, *Yorks. W.R.*
Risbridge, *Suff.*
Rochdale, *Lancs.*
Rochford, *Essex*
Romford, *Essex*
Romney Marsh, *Kent*
Romsey, *Hants.*
.Ross, *Heref.*
Rothbury, *Nhmbd.*
Rotherham, *Yorks. W.R.*
Rotherhithe, *London: Surrey*
Royston, *Herts.*
Rugby, *Warw.*
Runcorn, *Ches.*
Ruthin, *Denbs.*
Rye, *Sussex*

Saddleworth, *Yorks. W.R.*
Saffron Walden, *Essex*
St. -- see under name of Saint
Salford, *Lancs.*
Salisbury, *Wilts.*
Samford, *Suff.*
Saviour, St. (Southwark), *London: Surrey*
Scarborough, *Yorks. N.R.*
Sculcoates, *Yorks. E.R.*
Sedbergh, *Yorks. W.R.*
Sedgefield, *Dur.*
Seisdon, *Staffs.*
Selby, *Yorks. W.R.*
Settle, *Yorks. W.R.*
Sevenoaks, *Kent*
Shaftesbury, *Dorset*
Shardlow, *Dbys.*
Sheffield, *Yorks. W.R.*
Sheppey, *Kent*
Shepton Mallet, *Som.*
Sherborne, *Dorset*

Shields, South, *Dur.*
Shifnal, *Salop.*
Shipston on Stour, *Warw.*
Shoreditch, *London: Middx.*
Shrewsbury, *Salop.*
Skipton, *Yorks. W.R.*
Skirlaugh, *Yorks. E.R.*
Sleaford, *Lincs.*
Smallburgh, *Norf.*
Solihull, *Warw.*
Southam, *Warw.*
Southampton, *Hants.*
South Manchester, *Lancs.*
South Molton, *Devon*
South Shields, *Dur.*
South Stoneham, *Hants.*
Southwark, *London: Surrey*
Southwell, *Notts.*
Spalding, *Lincs.*
Spilsby, *Lincs.*
Stafford, *Staffs.*
Staines, *Middx.*
Stamford, *Lincs.*
Stepney, *London: Middx.*
Steyning, *Sussex*
Stockbridge, *Hants.*
Stockport, *Ches.*
Stockton, *Dur.*
Stoke Damerel, *Devon*
Stokesley, *Yorks. N.R.*
Stoke on Trent, *Staffs.*
Stone, *Staffs.*
Stoneham, South, *Hants.*
Stonehouse, East, *Devon*
Stourbridge, *Worcs.*
Stow, *Suff.*
Stow on the Wold, *Glos.*
Strand, *London: Middx.*
Stratford on Avon, *Warw.*
Stratton, *Corn.*
Strood, *Kent*
Stroud, *Glos.*
Sturminster, *Dorset*
Sudbury, *Suff.*
Sunderland, *Dur.*
Sutton, *Sussex*
Swaffham, *Norf.*
Swansea, *Glam.*
Swindon, *Wilts.*

Tadcaster, *Yorks. W.R.*
Tamworth, *Staffs.*
Tarvin, *Ches.*

Taunton, *Som.*
Tavistock, *Devon*
Teesdale, *Dur.*
Tenbury, *Worcs.*
Tendring, *Essex*
Tenterden, *Kent*
Tetbury, *Glos.*
Tewkesbury, *Glos.*
Thakeham, *Sussex*
Thame, *Oxon.*
Thanet, Isle of, *Kent*
Thetford, *Norf.*
Thingoe, *Suff.*
Thirsk, *Yorks. N.R.*
Thomas, St., *Devon*
Thornbury, *Glos.*
Thorne, *Yorks. W.R.*
Thrapston, *N'hants.*
Ticehurst, *Sussex*
Tisbury, *Wilts.*
Tiverton, *Devon*
Todmorden, *Lancs.*
Tonbridge, *Kent*
Torrington, *Devon*
Totnes, *Devon*
Towcester, *N'hants.*
Toxteth Park, *Lancs.*
Tregaron, *Cards.*
Trowbridge, *Wilts.*
Truro, *Corn.*
Tunstead, *Norf.*
Tynemouth, *Nhmbd.*

Uckfield, *Sussex*
Ulverstone, *Lancs.*
Uppingham, *Rutland*
Upton on Severn, *Worcs.*
Uttoxeter, *Staffs.*
Uxbridge, *Middx.*

Wakefield, *Yorks. W.R.*
Wallingford, *Berks.*
Walsall, *Staffs.*
Walsingham, *Norf.*
Wandsworth, *London: Surrey*
Wangford, *Suff.*
Wantage, *Berks.*
Ward, East, *Westmd.*
Ward, West, *Westmd.*
Ware, *Herts.*
Wareham, *Dorset*
Warminster, *Wilts.*
Warrington, *Lancs.*
Warwick, *Warw.*
Watford, *Herts.*
Wayland, *Norf.*
Weardale, *Dur.*
Wellingborough, *N'hants.*
Wellington, *Salop.*
Wellington, *Som.*
Wells, *Som.*
Welwyn, *Herts.*
Wem, *Salop.*

Weobley, *Heref.*
West Ashford, *Kent*
Westbourne, *Sussex*
West Bromwich, *Staffs.*
Westbury on Severn, *Glos.*
Westbury, *Wilts.*
West Derby, *Lancs.*
West Firle, *Sussex*
West Flegg, *Norf.*
West Ham, *Essex*
Westhampnett, *Sussex*
Westminster, *London: Middx.*
West Ward, *Westmd.*
Wetherby, *Yorks. W.R.*
Weymouth, *Dorset*
Wharfedale, *Yorks. W.R.*
Wheatenhurst, *Glos.*
Whitby, *Yorks. N.R.*
Whitchurch, *Hants.*
Whitchurch, *Salop.*
Whitechapel, *London: Middx.*
Whitehaven, *Cumbd.*
Whittlesey, *Cambs.*
Whorwelsdown, *Wilts.*
Wigan, *Lancs.*
Wight, Isle of, *Hants.*
Wigton or Wigtown, *Cumbs.*
Willesden, *Middx.*

Williton, *Som.*
Wilton, *Wilts.*
Wimborne, *Dorse*
Wincanton, *Som.*
Winchcombe, *Glo*
Winchester, *Hant*
Windsor, *Berks.*
Winslow, *Bucks.*
Winstree, *Essex*
Wirrall, *Ches.*
Wisbech, *Cambs*
Witham, *Essex*
Witney, *Oxon.*
Woburn, *Beds.*
Wokingham, *Ber*
Wolstanton, *Staf*
Wolverhampton,
Woodbridge, *Su*
Woodstock, *Oxo*
Woolwich, *Lond*
Kent
Wootton Bassett
Worcester, *Wor*
Worksop, *Notts.*
Wortley, *Yorks.*
Wrexham, *Denb*
Wycombe, *Buck*

Yarmouth, Grea
Yeovil, *Som.*
York, *Yorks. E.F*